WWW.DAVENPORTPRESS.ORG

GO TO

TO DOWNLOAD FORMS,

DOWNLOAD BOOKS,

AND GIVE COMMENTS

DAVENPORT'S PENNSYLVANIA WILLS AND ESTATE PLANNING LEGAL FORMS

Alexander William Russell

Ernest Charles Hope

Second Edition – 2015

Published by Davenport Press

ALSO PUBLISHED BY DAVENPORT PRESS

Davenport's Florida Wills And Estate Planning Legal Forms
Davenport's Georgia Wills And Estate Planning Legal Forms
Davenport's Illinois Wills And Estate Planning Legal Forms
Davenport's Indiana Wills And Estate Planning Legal Forms
Davenport's Maryland Wills And Estate Planning Legal Forms
Davenport's Massachusetts Wills And Estate Planning Legal Forms
Davenport's Michigan Wills And Estate Planning Legal Forms
Davenport's Minnesota Wills And Estate Planning Legal Forms
Davenport's Missouri Wills And Estate Planning Legal Forms
Davenport's Nebraska Wills And Estate Planning Legal Forms
Davenport's New Jersey Wills And Estate Planning Legal Forms
Davenport's New York Wills And Estate Planning Legal Forms
Davenport's North Carolina Wills And Estate Planning Legal Forms
Davenport's Ohio Wills And Estate Planning Legal Forms
Davenport's Tennessee Wills And Estate Planning Legal Forms
Davenport's Texas Wills And Estate Planning Legal Forms
Davenport's Wyoming Wills And Estate Planning Legal Forms

Booklet Series

Davenport's California Will And Estate Planning Legal Forms Booklet
Davenport's Maine Will And Estate Planning Legal Forms Booklet
Davenport's Wisconsin Will And Estate Planning Legal Forms Booklet

Accounting C.P.A. Series

Davenport's Federal Estate And Gift Tax 2015 Basic Forms Review
Davenport's Spreadsheet And Print Templates For 1099-MISC 2015

Publication Description:
Title: Davenport's Pennsylvania Wills And Estate Planning Legal Forms
Edition: Second, 2015
Authors: Alexander William Russell and Ernest Charles Hope
Publisher: **DAVENPORT PRESS,** 54 Amelia Ave., West St. Paul, MN 55118

THIS PUBLICATION IS NOT A SUBSTITUTE FOR LEGAL ADVICE.
Publisher and authors say, declare, and warn this publication is not to be considered the rendering of legal, accounting, or other professional services, which if wanted can be obtained from other sources and individuals.
No attorney-client or other relationship is agreed to or created by the purchase or use of this publication.

TABLE OF CONTENTS

CHAPTER 1
GUIDE TO BOOK AND FORMS

THIS BOOK HAS 10 FORMS BUT MOST PEOPLE ONLY USE A FEW FORMS

In this book 10 legal forms are provided that can make binding legal documents if completed, but most people only use a few of these forms. The legal forms in this book are:

Form 1. Last Will And Testament (With Guardians) (this form is a Will that lets people give property and control other issues after their death, and this form has a "Guardians" paragraph to name guardians to care for persons under 18 and their property in case this is ever needed);

Form 2. Last Will And Testament (No Guardians) (this is a Will form like Form 1 but with no paragraph on guardians and is for people with no child under 18 and not giving things to any minors);

Form 3. Self-Proving Affidavit (this form is often done with a Will to help the later process after a death of proving a Will was signed correctly, and this form makes it more likely a Will is followed);

Form 4. Tangible Personal Property List (lets people write down in lists outside a Will wanted gifts to occur on death of "tangible personal property" like clothes, furniture, vehicles, and jewelry);

Form 5. Codicil (this form can make changes to an existing Will, but most just do a new Will);

Form 6. Durable Health Care Power Of Attorney And Health Care Treatment Instructions (Living Will) (in case a person later can't control their health care this form lets a person name a "Health Care Agent" to control things (often a spouse or friend), and if wanted give health care orders);

Form 7. P.O.L.S.T. (Do Not Resuscitate) (this form which stands for "Pennsylvania Orders for Life-Sustaining Treatment" but is often called a Do Not Resuscitate tells paramedics and others not try to restart the heart or breathing (usually called C.P.R.) and certain other major actions);

Form 8. Durable Power of Attorney (this form lets power over a person's accounts, property, money, and more be shared with person like spouse or trusted friend to let them control and do things);

Form 9. Medical Consent Authorization (For Child) (this form lets parent give power over a child's medical care to someone to let them control this to help or because parents may be away); and

Form 10. Statement Of Contrary Intent (For Body) (rather than as normal a person's closest family controlling the dead body and funeral and burial, this form lets a "contrary intent" than this be said and an agent and instructions be given for this).

1

BOOK REVIEWS LAW AND HAS GOOD RANGE OF LEGAL FORMS

This book covers Pennsylvania Wills and Estate Planning legal documents which deal with how a person can act now to control upon illness or death their health care, end of life issues, property, money, children, funeral and burial, and other matters. This book provides in one convenient place a quick review of some law and many ready to use legal forms that make binding legal documents. To reduce confusion and skimming by people this book is short and quickly shows legal forms, and people who later want can easily get more information from other places. Pennsylvania law applies if people live here more than temporarily. This book is written to give people information and options.

BOOK AND FORMS SHOULD BE SUFFICIENT IF ONE HAS USUAL SITUATION

This book and its legal forms cannot cover everything or all possible legal complications but should be sufficient for people with usual situations and wishes. Wills and Estate Planning forms actually do simple things. This book discusses many legal areas to show often no special action is needed. Half this book's forms are not even by a lawyer but are standard forms (with instructions or written to be self-explanatory) by the state legislature, by a state agency, or with basic words to match a state law.

PEOPLE WITH UNUSUAL SITUATIONS OR WISHES MAY NEED A LAWYER

Some people may need a lawyer for Wills and Estate Planning documents especially those with unusual wishes or situations, like 1) wealth over $2 million, 2) complex family situations, 3) unusual wishes for gifts, or 4) big family medical concerns (like persons with long-term care or special needs). But using a lawyer can take several visits over months, costs $1000-$3000 a person, and results from lawyers vary (and some forms are redone every 3-5 years raising costs about ten-fold over a lifetime). In life people must often weigh the likely costs and benefits and decide whether to pay a lawyer. Most people have not used a lawyer for a Will and similar documents. Often Will and Estate Planning documents are not vital but just save small costs and work, or avoid problems with basic words any standard form has, or these documents are never used or not used for decades. People often don't use lawyers even for bigger things like some accidents, home or car buying, jobs, loans, financial planning, and family problems. Many people dislike that lawyers cost so much or the law is allowed to be or at least seem so complex. **This book is not a substitute for legal advice and no lawyer-client relationship is created by this book.**

SOME DOCUMENTS NOT IN THIS BOOK ARE LESS COMMONLY USED

This book does not contain some legal documents that are less commonly used.

Property and debt lists are informally written each year by some people to help after their death.

"Revocable Living Trust" papers may be suggested to transfer item by item most of a person's things into a trust for years, mainly to have property transfer faster after a death and save small costs and maybe avoid probate, but this is rarely done and can make living and paperwork difficult for years.

"Childrens Trust" papers to have a trust manage a minor's property and money may be suggested, but a Will names a "guardian of the estate" to manage and spend a minor's things for them until age 18, and trusts mainly are done just to avoid small yearly costs of a court review that helps avoid misuse.

"Standby Guardian" forms can be done to try to have power over children quickly go to someone if a parent dies or falls badly ill, but a court hearing must confirm this and a Will already names guardians.

"Organ Donation" forms are not usually done separately but in other forms like for a drivers license, state ID, or other forms (like this book's Form 6). People can also sign up at the Department of Transportation at www.dot.state.pa.us. A person's family can later consent to organ donation if a person in life did not say this was not wanted.

DOWNLOAD OR PHOTOCOPY FORMS AND RARELY CHANGE FORMS

To get forms people can 1) download forms free as this book's Appendix A explains how to do, or 2) photocopy pages from this book. Book pages that are forms do not have bottom page numbers. When filling out forms people can use a computer or just handwrite to add words, but people should be sure to handwrite signatures and nearby dates in permanent ink. Most forms clearly show with blank spaces and underlining where to add words and signatures (like, "I name _____ as Agent"). This book also shows several ways to change words or add legal language in forms, but making big changes to forms is not usually needed and can be risky and is not recommended.

MANY PEOPLE SKIP SOME OF THIS BOOK AND SKIP USING MOST FORMS

This book goes into many legal details and explains many legal forms that may not interest most people. Skipping reading some of this book is not recommended but probably won't harm normal people with usual situations or wishes. Skipping using some of this book's forms is recommended and most people only use 3 to 5 book forms. For example, many people only do a Will like in Form 1, a Self-Proving Affidavit like Form 3, and a health care form like Form 6, and skip using other forms.

CHAPTER 2
BASIC TERMS AND LAW

SOME IDEAS AND WORDS ARE BASIC TO WILLS AND ESTATE PLANNING

Some ideas and words are basic to Wills and Estate Planning law and forms.

■ <u>A person who has died is called a "decedent" or "deceased".</u>

■ A "Will" is a document done by a person to control some issues after their death. A Will is often called a "Last Will And Testament" and anyone doing a Will is called "Testator".

■ "Property" is anything of value and is either 1) "real property" which is land, buildings, and fixtures attached to land or buildings, or 2) "personal property" which is any other property like money, accounts, investments, jewelry, clothing, furniture, appliances, equipment, vehicles, and anything else.

■ A "beneficiary" is a person getting things without fully paying, like from a gift in a Will.

■ "Heir" is a person who gets property on a death due to a Will or state law (they "inherit").

■ "Probate" is a legal process that may help with issues after a person's death, and it can help transfer property, pick guardians, show everyone things were done fairly, handle creditors, and more. Pennsylvania probate unlike some states is fairly fast and affordable and also has simpler options.

■ An "Executor" (also called a "Personal Representative") is the person in charge of any probate process and other things after a death, and often is a spouse, adult child, or friend.

■ "Notary" (also called a "notary public") is a person approved by the state to make signing of certain documents more official, and they can be found at banks, insurance agents, court, some copy places, or (often best to avoid delay and bother) can be hired from the phonebook.

■ The word "respectively" means "in the order just said" and often is used near where people sign.

■ Pennsylvania laws are called "statutes" or "sections" and are grouped in "chapters" and finally in "titles" (Title 20, the "Probate, Estates & Fiduciaries Code" or "PEF Code", is often used). A state law is often called "Consolidated" which just means renumbered. Pennsylvania law is usually cited like "20 Pa.C.S.A. § 101", with "§" meaning section and "A" meaning it is in a book with "annotated" notes. Pennsylvania law can be looked up free in the online "Purdon's" books from the Westlaw company. Various court rules may also apply. Federal law is found in the U.S. Code.

■ A form put in law by state legislators to help people (or as a sample) is called a "statutory form".

■ Wills and related issues usually involve the "Orphan's Court" clerk who is housed in the local and useful "Register of Wills" office, both of which are located in the "Court of Common Pleas".

"ESTATE" MEANS PROPERTY OF DECEDENT OR A BODY MANAGING THINGS

Property of a decedent that on death did not transfer automatically to other owners is called the "estate" of a decedent, or the "probate estate". Also after a death there may be an "estate" body run by an executor to do things and temporarily hold property, and a decedent's accounts and other property might be renamed for a few months like "Estate of [decedent]".

"NON-PROBATE PROPERTY" TRANSFERS AS ARRANGED NOT BY WILL

Importantly, property that for some reason automatically transfers on a death to other owners is called "non-probate property" and such property transfers as arranged even if a Will names the property. Examples are a) "beneficiary" forms name someone to get accounts or other things, b) property is held by several as "joint tenants", c) life insurance names a person as beneficiary, or d) transfer-on-death or pay-on-death accounts are used. Arranging non-probate transfers is called "avoiding probate" if done for most things, but this is rare since it can make living and paperwork difficult for years just to save others small work and costs. Basically, when doing a Will people should consider non-probate transfers that may occur and plan accordingly.

OWNERSHIP OF PROPERTY DETERMINES WHAT CAN BE GIFTED

A person can only gift by Will or other way property and money they own, and many rules affect this.

Very basically, in Pennsylvania a person usually owns all they earn, and also owns things or parts of things their resources contribute the funds to get or improve.

Pennsylvania is not a "community property" state (like California or Texas) where a spouse owns half a spouse's income and gains (but things from when living in such states may stay owned 50/50).

A person owns inheritances and gifts made to them even if married or if they have children.

People can anytime change owners by doing an agreement, gifting, or failing to keep track of things.

For property with title documents (real estate or vehicles) or where people list owners (like accounts) listed persons are owners unless people can prove a mistake, an agreement to share or return, or they worked or gave resources to get or improve things not as a gift and legally they should be owners.

There are many ways several people can own the same property, most often as "tenants in common" with a 50% or other share they can sell or gift in life and then on death it goes as a Will says.

A person in life is free to make gifts or sell property even property named in a Will, and family often say a person verbally gave them some needed things in life so they get the things.

Basically, people doing a Will should review paperwork and ask questions to see what they own and can gift in a Will or other ways.

REAL ESTATE IS OWNED AS TITLE PAPERS SAY WHICH CAN LIMIT GIFTING

Real estate is usually owned how title papers say, which can limit power to transfer in life or by Will:

a) normal or "separate" ownership usually occurs if just 1 person is listed on title, then the owner usually has power to sell or gift during life and to gift by Will;

b) "tenants in common" may occur if several are listed on title, then an owner has a percent share (like 50%) they can sell or gift in life or gift by Will (this is a common way of owning many things);

c) "joint tenant with right of survivorship" occurs if several are named on title and this is said, then an owner has a percent share like 50% they can sell or gift during life but can't gift by Will since on death it goes to other named owners (this is how married couples often own the family house);

d) a "life estate" occurs if title papers say so, then usually 1 person uses a property for their life but can't sell or gift in life or gift by Will since on death the property goes to others named on the title; and

e) "trust property" occurs when paperwork creates a trust and people item by item transferred property into it, then only a "trustee" in charge can sell or gift trust property in ways the trust allows, and Wills can't usually affect trust property even if a Will maker use to own the property in the trust.

Pennsylvania does not use "tenants by the entirety" type of ownership for married people or others. Property not real estate (like accounts) can be owned in these complex ways or by many people too.

IF THERE IS NO WILL THEN STATE "INTESTATE" LAW TRANSFERS PROPERTY

"Intestate" means to die with no Will. If there is no Will then "intestate law" says what happens to "estate property" (property that did not transfer automatically on death). Intestate law says any spouse gets the first $30,000 plus 1/2 the rest (this $30,000 is skipped if any child of a decedent comes from another relationship). The remaining half (or everything is there is no spouse) goes to the first living of the following: descendants (children, or grandchildren who take in a dead parent's place), parents, brothers and sisters, and then other close family. Only if all this fails does the state get things.

BEFORE DEBTS OR WILL A FAMILY CAN GET $3,500 "FAMILY EXEMPTION"

Before most creditors are paid and before a Will is carried out "family exemption" law gives family the right to $3,500 of money or property of a decedent. This right goes to any spouse and then to children or parents who lived with a decedent even if adults. No tax and most payments to creditors comes before a family exemption, except some funeral, burial, probate, and last illness debts do have priority to be paid first. Paying the family exemption uses some property and money of a decedent so may interfere with Will gifts, but helpfully if family in a Will get most things they often skip this. <u>Basically, people doing a Will should consider if family may use exemption rights to claim $3,500 of things first.</u>

DEBTS ARE PAID BEFORE WILL GIFTS BUT NOT MORTGAGES OR LIENS

Creditors a decedent owed usually are paid before Will gifts are carried out, like a decedent's bills, loans, credit cards, and debts owed to family and friends. Paying creditors uses some of a decedent's property and money so could interfere with Will gifts which people should plan for. To pay debts:

1) first used is property passing by Will residue clause (which is property no other Will part used),

2) next used to pay debts are things in Will "general gifts" (like plain gifts of money), and

3) last used to pay debts is property in Will specific gifts (where property is specifically described).

To pay creditors non-probate transfers of property or money can be undone if all other property has been used up. But state law does not usually pay off secured debts like mortgages or car liens, so people who get such property by Will or other way must keep paying such debts to keep the property. Wills can be changed to say secured debts should be paid, like "Before gifts in this Will occur all debts on my 1989 Buick and my property at 9 Rex Rd., Ivy, PA, is to be paid off". A simpler option is to just give money to help pay a mortgage or lien. Family need not themselves usually pay debts they didn't co-sign or guarantee.

SPOUSE RATHER THAN FOLLOW WILL CAN CHOOSE "ELECTIVE SHARE"

State law says a spouse unhappy with what a Will gives them can instead elect an "Elective Share" of 1/3 of some property of a decedent. This law is based on fairness and to avoid a spouse having to divorce to be certain of money for old age rather than stay married. The Elective Share is 1/3 the following: decedent's estate property and money, things gifted away in last year over $3,000 a person, things transferred where decedent still kept some rights, or some things a decedent could take back or which might return like jointly owned property. But the Elective Share might not affect certain "non-probate transfers" that transfer property automatically to others or most life insurance or most employee benefits, and a spouse worried about this may want to see a lawyer. Since paying an Elective Share uses some of a decedent's property and money this may interfere with Will gifts, but to the degree possible others not a spouse still follow a Will. <u>Basically, people doing a Will usually give well over 1/3 of their property and money to any spouse to avoid them wanting an Elective Share.</u> In rare cases a lawyer prenuptial or postnuptial contract spouses sign can give up Elective Share rights.

DO NEW WILL IF DIVORCE, MARRY, HAVE NEW CHILD, OR MOVE STATES

Divorcing, marrying, having a new child, or moving to a new state after writing a Will can have big legal effects. If any of these occur it is recommended people do a new Will and review other papers.

AFTER A DEATH OCCURS THERE ARE SEVERAL PROBATE OPTIONS

Pennsylvania normal probate is fairly fast and affordable and often takes around 6 months unlike some other states. There are also some easier less formal probate options and most Wills allow these.

A "Small Estate" process that skips most probate steps and takes a couple months can be done if a decedent's estate has under $50,000 of property and money left in it (up from $25,000 in 2013).

Savings institutions and most pre-paid health accounts can release up to $10,000 to family.

Life insurance companies can release up to $11,000 to family (or more if the insurance names living people as beneficiaries and does not name the estate or the deceased).

An employer can pay up to $5,000 of unpaid wages to family.

Vehicles usually can be re-titled by using title forms at the state department of transportation.

By law safe deposit boxes can be looked into by a bank for a Will or related documents.

Non-probate transfers often can be completed by showing of a death certificate, such as for land held with a joint tenant, transfer-on-death accounts, or any investment that has a named beneficiary.

But "Ancillary Probate" is a costly proceeding in another state needed for property there (usually real property), but this cost may be avoided by holding property in another state jointly with a person.

USUALLY LITTLE FEDERAL OR PENNSYLVANIA TAX IS OWED ON A DEATH

Usually little tax is owed due to a death to the Federal government, other states, or Pennsylvania.

First, the "Federal Estate And Gift Tax" taxes some transfers made in life or that occur on death, but this only starts when a tax credit is used up that covers $5,430,000 in transfers in or after 2015.

Second, another state's estate or inheritance tax can be owed for things located there or going to persons there, but just 15 states have such taxes and they usually start at over $2,000,000.

Third, a "Pennsylvania Inheritance Tax" might apply but it usually costs little since the rate depends on a recipient's relationship, from a) 0% for a spouse, b) 4.5% for descendants or ancestors (like children or parents), c) 12% for brothers and sisters, and d) 15% for all others. For example, gifts to a spouse, a child, and a brother of $10,000 each trigger, in order, tax of just $0, $450, and $1,200.

Unless a Will says otherwise property passing by a Will's residue clause is used to pay taxes on Will gifts, but people getting gifts outside a Will pay any tax themselves. No tax is owed for most life insurance received or most gifts to a church or charity. For tax purposes property often can be valued low if normal buyers would not offer much to come and transport away used household items of unknown condition. Tax officials rarely notice if household or similar items are not listed on tax forms.

CHAPTER 3
BASIC ISSUES IN WILLS AND GIFTING

"WILL" IS DOCUMENT OFTEN DONE TO CONTROL ISSUES AFTER DEATH

A "Will" is a legal document that can be done by a person of sound mind at least age 18 to control many issues that may arise after their death. Issues in a Will can include who gets money and property, who will manage things as executor, if faster legal procedures can be used, and who if needed will be guardians of minor children under 18 and of any minor's property. Not doing a Will can cause confusion, more costs, hearings, delay, and family fights. A Will is often called a "Last Will And Testament" and the person doing a Will is called "Testator".

WILLS ARE USUALLY SIGNED BEFORE 2 WITNESSES WHO ALSO SIGN

Normally a Will is signed by a person before 2 witnesses who then sign too. State law does let Wills be done without witnesses signing, but this is rare and then later when trying to enforce a Will 2 persons who saw the signing must testify convincingly or other proof is needed. Not having 2 witnesses sign causes delay, increases costs, and makes a Will less far likely to be followed. Persons who act as the 2 witnesses who sign can be family, can be named executor or guardian, and can be getting Will gifts, but it is a bit better if people without these connections are used as witnesses. To reduce forgery or attempts to add a page to a Will some people modify a Will to have places to initial each page, but this is not legally required and is not standard.

WILL CAN BE SUPPORTED BY SELF-PROVING AFFIDAVIT

A Will can be supported by a "Self-Proving Affidavit" signed before a notary. This is explained further in this book's Chapter 6 which has this book's Form 3, the "Self-Proving Affidavit" form.

LISTS OUTSIDE A WILL CAN GIVE "TANGIBLE PERSONAL PROPERTY"

Pennsylvania law lets people write in lists separate from a Will any wanted later gifts of tangible personal property like household items, jewelry, and clothing. This is explained further in this book's Chapter 7 which has this book's Form 4, the "Tangible Personal Property List" form.

WILL CAN BE REVOKED BY NEW WILL, TEARING UP, OR MARKING

To cancel or "revoke" a Will a person can do a new Will which says it revokes previous Wills, or can personally do acts showing intent to revoke like tearing up, burning, or writing "canceled" on pages. Revoking a Will does not usually bring back into force earlier Wills.

IN WILL CAN NAME "EXECUTOR" TO HANDLE MATTERS AFTER DEATH

Most Wills name an "executor" to if needed do things after a death like manage probate, find and transfer property and money, do paperwork, and pay bills. A person named executor in a Will often is a spouse, adult child, or friend (or a lawyer or bank if they agree), and they can live outside the state. Executors can be getting Will gifts and can be named as guardian in a Will. If needed and no Will names an executor a judge in a costly long hearing picks from a spouse and family who may argue. Naming 2 persons to be executor at the same time is rarer due to possible legal problems and delays. Executors are paid back for any fees and costs they pay. An executor can ask to be paid for their work as executor and most judges follow the "Johnson Estate" formula that starts at 5% of estate property and then decreases with estate size, but asking for pay is often skipped as this uses up estate assets and is taxable income. State law also calls an executor a "Personal Representative".

IF USED A LAWYER FOR EXECUTOR IS PAID USING ESTATE PROPERTY

Sometimes an executor can go without a lawyer, but if needed or wanted a lawyer is paid for using decedent's estate money and property. A lawyer is usually paid what an executor agrees to, and often is about $150/hour or a total fee of about $3,000 which is low given the big amounts maybe involved.

EXECUTOR HAS POWER TO EASILY COLLECT AND TRANSFER PROPERTY

An executor by law has power to easily collect and transfer most property and money of a decedent. Banks, investment companies, and others will usually follow instructions of an executor. Most Wills also have a part where executors are given more powers to help them do things.

WILL CAN NAME "GUARDIAN OF THE PERSON" TO CARE FOR CHILDREN

If a parent dies with a child under 18 the other natural or adopted parent (but not a step-parent) takes over automatically unless found "unfit" by a court which is rare. But in case it is ever needed a parent in a Will can name a "guardian of the person" to care for a child under 18, which choice a court follows unless a person clearly is not suitable. State law says preference of a "sole surviving parent" (so the last parent to die) is given more weight. If needed and no Will names a guardian a judge in a costly long hearing picks from family who may argue about this. Naming 2 persons to be guardian at the same time is less common due to likely arguments and legal issues even if they are married. Basically, in a Will since naming the other parent as guardian of the person is pointless (they take over unless unfit) most people name for this a healthy relative or friend. People without a child under 18 can skip or fill in a guardian clause anyway, or use a Will without this like this book's Form 2.

WILL CAN NAME "GUARDIAN OF THE ESTATE" FOR A MINOR'S PROPERTY

In a Will a "guardian of the estate" can be named to manage property and money of those under 18 and decide how to use these to help pay for health care, schools, and living costs until they are no longer minors when anything left is handed over. By law persons under 18 can own but cannot control major property, and banks and others may refuse to deal with minors in large matters. Courts follow a parent's choice for guardian of the estate unless a person clearly is not suitable. If needed and no Will names a guardian of the estate a judge in a costly long hearing picks from a parent and family who may argue. Naming 2 persons to be guardian at the same time is less common due to likely arguments and legal issues even if they are married. Often the person who is "guardian of the person" is also named guardian of the estate unless they are bad with money (this avoids arguments and they know what should be paid for). <u>Basically, usually when naming a guardian of the estate in a Will either 1) a minor will likely get things when a parent is still alive so the parent is named for this, or 2) a minor will likely get things only if all parents are dead so a friend or relative is named for this</u>. Those without children under 18 and not giving things to any minors can skip or fill in anyway a guardian of the estate clause, or use a Will without this like this book's Form 2.

DUE TO COSTS AND HASSLE MANY PEOPLE AVOID GIFTING TO MINORS

A guardian of the estate (which was just talked about above) does face extra work and costs to manage and spend a minor's property, and also each year there a court review looking for misuse. Due to this extra work and costs many people avoid gifting to persons under 18. Or some people gift to minors via family, like "I give $80 to Ann Mary Fox in the hope she will help her son Leo Oliver Fox". But a helpful new law, the Uniform Transfers To Minors Act, says a "custodian" process with less costs and work can manage a minor's property, and often Wills says a guardian of the estate can act like a custodian to avoid most work and costs (this book's Wills do this).

WILL CAN HAVE "ALTERNATE" EXECUTOR OR GUARDIANS BUT THIS IS RARE

If a person named in a Will as executor or guardian dies or is unavailable most people can just write a new Will or a judge will pick someone to serve if needed. But to plan ahead for the rare case someone named executor or guardian dies or is unavailable people can modify a Will to name an "alternate" person, which is done by adding after a name:

"or if they are reasonably unable to serve I nominate ___ to serve".

WILLS CAN SKIP EXECUTOR "BOND" AND ALLOW INFORMAL PROBATE

Most Wills say no "bond" or "surety" is required. This is insurance against executor misconduct paid for using some estate funds, but most people do not want this cost since the executor is trusted. By saying no bond is required a Will can let an executor living outside the state not need a bond. Most Wills also say informal and less costly probate options should be used if possible.

WILLS USE NORMAL WORDS TO TRANSFER MOST THINGS AFTER DEATH

A Will is the normal way a person says what happens to their property and money after their death. To do gifts in a Will often very simple words are used, like "I give _____ to _____", and the law no longer requires words like "devise", "bequeath", or "legacy". A Will gift need not be written perfectly so long if after all evidence (including hearing from people who knew a decedent) the likely meaning of a Will gift can be seen.

IN A WILL CAN DO SPECIFIC GIFTS TO GIFT PARTICULAR PROPERTY

Most Wills in their main area have many "Specific Gift" sentences to let people gift particular property to persons who are named. Specific gifts can be any kind of property like clothing, jewelry, furniture, tools, cars, investments, accounts, and real estate. Specific gifts are given some preference and are carried out before most other Will gifts, and if possible the law tries to pay a decedent's debts and family rights not using things in specific gifts. Examples of specific gifts are:

"I give Tin Cups to Jo Dodd",

"I give UBank account ending in 8473 to Ivy Dee",

"I give all clothing to Ann Coe",

"I give 1988 Ford truck and 2 broken trailers to Jerry Smith and Eric Blitzer", and

"I give 291 Blue Lake Road, Kilby, TX, including all land, buildings, and fixtures to Ann Jo Knox".

IN A WILL CAN DO GENERAL GIFTS OF MONEY AMOUNTS

Many people in a Will give "general gifts" which are any gifts not involving specific property and usually are money. An example of a Will money gift is, "I give $500 to Kevin Jones". Later an executor will have power to use money in accounts or sell property to carry out money gifts. Even if a Will gifts money a person can still agree with an executor to take some property instead. Money gifts are often written with a Will's specific gifts but legally they are different. For money gifts to several people, "I give $90 to Ben Lee and Jan Kim" means the same as "I give a total of $90 to Ben Lee and Jan Kim", but using the words "total" or "each" can help avoid confusion.

"RESIDUE CLAUSE" IN WILL HELPFULLY GIVES ANYTHING LEFT OVER

Most Wills have a "residue clause" towards their end that gives any property and money of a person not used by other Will parts or by other means to persons named. This "catch-all" ensures everything goes to someone. Many people use a residue clause to give most their things since this has less legal risks and avoids having to describe property. Often a Will's residue clause has:

1) a 1st space to name 1 or more persons to get things if they are living at the Will maker's death (many name a spouse or closest family here), and

2) a 2nd space to name people to get things if all in the 1st space don't survive (due to Will wording the share of anyone named in the 2nd space who don't survive usually goes to their descendants).

People should consider if debts to be paid, earlier gifts in a Will, and any non-probate transfers may leave little for a residue clause to give.

WILLS GIFTS USUALLY ARE CARRIED OUT IN A CERTAIN ORDER

When Will gifts are carried out by law they usually occur in a certain order, which is:

1) Will "specific gifts" that name particular property are done first,

2) Will "general gifts" like money amounts are done next, and then

3) the Will "residue" gift is done last (which is basically anything remaining).

Gifts of the same type usually occur in the order written in a Will. People should consider if gifts carried out earlier may leave less for later Will gifts.

WILL GIFTS NOT OF MONEY BUT OF PROPERTY ARE RISKIER

Will gifts not of money but of property can change and even fail for many reasons, like a) property changed in value so the recipient gets far less value, b) property is claimed by family using legal rights like "family exemption" or "elective share" rights, c) property is sold or given away by a person before death so is no longer available to give, or d) property has to be sold to pay a decedent's debts. For many reasons in a Will rather than gift property it may be better to gift money or, also, may be better to gift using a Will "residue" clause (which gives all remaining property to persons named).

"CONDITIONS" CAN BE PUT ON A GIFT THAT MUST BE MET

"Conditions" can be put on a gift so if something does not occur the gift does not occur, like "I give all jewelry to Sue Lott if she loses 50 pounds" or "I give $90 to Amy Pond if she starts college". But gift conditions if strange or not of limited time can lead to delay, lawsuits, and hurt feelings. Gift conditions against public policy like if based on race or if too restrictive might be ignored.

THAT BENEFICIARY MUST "SURVIVE" TO GET GIFT IS USUAL CONDITION

Most Will gifts say "if they survive me" which means for a gift to occur the named beneficiary must be alive at the Will maker's death. A gift of no effect due to someone not surviving leaves the gifted property to follow later Will parts like a residue clause. To avoid legal problems most Wills define "survive" as outliving the Will maker by 60 days. If survival is not a gift condition then who gets a gift if a beneficiary has died depends on complex state law but sometimes it is the beneficiary's children.

ALTHOUGH RARELY NEEDED "ALTERNATE BENEFICIARY" CAN BE ADDED

For beneficiaries named to get Will gifts usually 1) they survive to get the gift, 2) they don't survive but this is seen and a Will is rewritten, or 3) they don't survive and survival was listed as a gift condition so property then goes to who a person chose in a Will's residue clause (often this is a spouse or child). But if wanted a person can name an "alternate beneficiary" to get a gift if the named beneficiary does not survive as required. This is done in a gift by removing "if they survive me" and adding, "but if they fail to survive me then to _____", like "I give $90 to Ed Dee but if they fail to survive me then to Jo Wu".

FAMILY CAN BE ALTERNATE BENEFICIARY USING "LINEAL DESCENDANTS"

Although rarely needed (as explained above) a person can have a beneficiary's descendants (like children or grandchildren) be alternate beneficiaries in case the person doesn't survive to get a gift. This can be done by removing "if they survive me" gift language and adding there "or their lineal descendants per stirpes". The phrase "per stirpes" in the Latin language means "by the root" and means property is split among family branches with younger generations take for a dead parent. A spouse is not a "descendant" so this language does not benefit anyone's spouse. An example is:

A man named Abe has 2 children Viv and Mort each of whom have 2 children. If Abe and Mort die and Abe's Will says "to Viv and Mort or lineal descendants per stirpes" the result is Viv gets 50% and Mort's 2 children each get 25%.

SEVERAL PERSONS CAN GET SAME PROPERTY OR MONEY TO SHARE

The same property or money can be gifted to several people to share, like "I give AmBank account ending in 8483 to Ed Coe and Jill Hill". Importantly, most Wills say for a gift to several persons if any have not survived other beneficiaries of the same gift take the non-survivor's share. So, "I give $90 to Jan, Ada, and Kay Smith if they survive me" usually means if Ada has died the other 2 persons get $45. Most Wills say a gift will be sold and money passed on if beneficiaries don't agree how to use or sell it.

14

BENEFICIARIES CAN GET PERCENTAGE RATHER THAN EQUAL SHARE

When several people are given the same Will gift this usually means they get an equal share, but if wanted a percentage can be written in to give such a share. Often a Will's "residue clause" is gifted by percentages to get the exact split wanted. Examples of Will gifts using percentages are:

"I give all tools 70% to Ed Coe and 30% to Max Dodd",

"I give 372 Lake Road, Knox, PA, 60% to Tom Dee and 40% to Ned Bund", and

'I give the residue 70% to Janet Ann Nox my wife, 20% to John Eric Nox, and 10% to Kay Ann Hill".

WILLS NEED SUFFICIENT DESCRIPTIONS OF PERSONS LIKE A FULL NAME

The person doing a Will usually should use their full legal name in all places including when signing. Some people add they are known by another name but this is not required (like, "I am also known as Big Smith" or "a/k/a Big Smith"). Those getting Will gifts must be described well enough so an executor after listening to people who knew a decedent and looking at circumstances can tell who likely is meant. A Will gift with a first and last name is usually enough with any added middle name and any "Junior" helping, but often a nickname is fine too. Family in a Will are usually called by their normal names. It may help to say how a person is known, like "from school", "my aunt", and "my New York friend". People can call up a charity to get the official name or people can just explain how the charity is known (like "the local animal shelter" or "my old church"). Wills can skip names if who is in a group is clear, like "I give $90 to each of my sister Kim's kids". Some people give a pet and money for pet care to a friend (like, "I give my cat Bo and $90 to Jo Dee") or get a lawyer's "Pet Trust". Examples of names in Wills are:

"I give $95 to Tom Smith my mechanic",

"I give my boat to Big Bjorg, Mary Smith, and Greg Paul Coe Jr.", and

"I give $800 to Bloomington Happy Meals a food charity in my county".

WILLS NEED SUFFICIENT DESCRIPTIONS OF PROPERTY GIFTED

Property in Will gifts must be described so those who knew a decedent can tell the likely meaning. This is easy as most people only own 1 of something to give. It is also OK to describe property by category, by standard location, or to have a long list of property in a single gift. For real property using a correct "legal description" is best (like "Lot 2, Block 4 of Polk's Addition to Boyd") but using a street address to give real property is allowed. Examples of describing property in Will gifts are:

"I give Ubank account ending #9283 to Mary Bing",

"I give tools usually kept in my garage and my biggest gold ring to Vera Kline", and

"I give 92 Lake Street, Ajax, Pennsylvania, including land, buildings, and fixtures, to Ann Joy Nox".

WILLS IGNORE PLURAL AND GENDER OF WORDS

Most Wills say plural or gender meanings of words are ignored which lets one put in spaces any thing wanted. So Wills use "they" when it may refer to 1 person, like "I give ___ to __ if they survive me".

WILLS HAVE LONG "MISCELLANEOUS" SECTION TO HELP AVOID PROBLEMS

Most Wills have a long "Miscellaneous" section with many sentences of legal language that help avoid some possible legal problems and which help explain parts of the Will.

KEEP SIGNED WILL IN SAFE PLACE IT CAN BE FOUND AFTER DEATH

When signed a Will should be stapled together and kept in a safe place where it can be found within days of a death, like in a desk, filing cabinet, safe or safe deposit box (if possible share access), or with a trusted person like spouse or friend (or tell them where to look). If a Will cannot be found and no one can say it was revoked or canceled this can create legal problems.

IN GENERAL GIFT AS WANTED, KEEP IT SIMPLE, AND CONSIDER A SPOUSE

In general it is often best to keep gifting in a Will simple. For example, it may be best in a Will to make a few small gifts (gifts of money not property may have less legal problems), and then use a Will's residue clause to give all else to 1 person or a few people. Some people just give everything to a spouse or another person who they trust to pass on property in ways discussed with them earlier. If a person has a spouse usually they are given most things in a Will or other ways because they may need this to live on and to avoid legal problems. If people later survive a spouse they can just do a new Will that switches to giving more to other persons. In Pennsylvania a person is mostly free to gift their property and money as they want including giving nothing to a child.

CHAPTER 4
FORM 1: LAST WILL AND TESTAMENT (WITH GUARDIANS)

FORM 1 IS A FLEXIBLE WILL WITH A GUARDIANS PARAGRAPH

Form 1 is a flexible Will that lets people write in what gifts of property and money they want to occur after their death. The Will in Form 1 also has a "Guardians" paragraph to let a person name a "guardian of the person" to if needed care for a child under 18, and name a "guardian of the estate" to if needed manage any minor's money or property. People with no child under 18 and also not giving anything to a person under 18 when at the Guardians paragraph can skip it, fill it in anyway, or use the Will in Form 2 without this paragraph. A Will is often called a "Last Will and Testament" and the person doing a Will is called "Testator".

WILL IN FORM 1 HAS BASIC LAYOUT WITH SEVERAL PARTS TO FILL OUT

The Will in Form 1 has a basic layout with several parts for a person to fill out to use.

At its start the Will has a place for a person making the Will to put their full legal name and county.

The 1st paragraph, "Gifts", has many spaces for a person to a) make specific gifts by a person describing particular property and naming persons to get these things, and b) make money gifts by a person writing in money amounts and naming persons to get this money.

The 2nd paragraph, "Tangible Personal Property List", just says to follow any gift lists people write.

The 3rd paragraph, "Residue", gives any property and money not used by other parts of the Will or in other ways, which is done by writing here the names of persons to get this.

The 4th paragraph, "Administration", has a space to write in someone's name to be "executor" to if needed handle most matters after a person's death, and often named is a spouse, child, or friend.

The 5th paragraph, "Guardians", has a space to name someone "guardian of the person" to if needed care for a child under 18, and to name someone "guardian of the estate" to if needed manage property and money of any minor and spend this on them until they are an adult and get anything left.

The 6th paragraph, "Miscellaneous", just has many sentences of legal language that help avoid certain legal problems and help explain the Will.

Last is where the Will maker signs their full name and 2 witnesses sign and write their addresses.

As just explained, the Will parts let people gift specific property and money, say any gift lists should be followed, gift the residue, name an executor, name guardians, and sign the end to make it valid.

RESIDUE CLAUSE HAS 2 PLACES TO NAME PEOPLE TO GET ANYTHING LEFT

In a Will's "residue clause" anything not used by other parts of the Will or other means is gifted to the persons named in the residue clause. A residue clause is a "catch-all" making sure all property and money goes to someone, or many people use the residue clause to gift most of their things. The residue clause in this book's Wills is written to have:

    1) a 1st space to name 1 or more persons to get the residue (but anyone named here must survive to get things or their share goes to others named here), and

    2) a 2nd space to name people to get things if all in the 1st space don't survive (any named here who don't survive have their share go to descendants due to language used in the Will).

Most people name in the 1st space a spouse or closest family and in the 2nd space name their next closest family or friends. Helpful special options exist which many people can use:

    a) People can in the residue clause leave the 1st space empty and only name people in the 2nd space to ensure if someone named dies their descendants get their share;

    b) People can repeat names in the 2 clause spaces if there is only 1 person or group to target; and

    c) People can in either of the residue clause's spaces gift using percentages.

This may seem complex but whoever is named in the 1st used space gets things if they survive.

WILL IS DONE BY PERSON SIGNING BEFORE 2 WITNESSES WHO SIGN TOO

A Will to be completed should be signed by the person doing the Will before 2 witnesses who then sign too. Everyone signing should be present and watch others sign. It is optional but before signing some people doing a Will hold it up and say to witnesses things like, "This is the Will I want and want you to witness". Before signing most witnesses read quietly to themselves the paragraph they sign, and witnesses need not read or have read to them the entire Will. In paragraphs that are signed there are places to add some names and dates, and this can be done by the person signing or beforehand by anyone. Last is a spot for witnesses to write their addresses just in case needed later. Witnesses should be at least 18 but if possible young enough to be available later if needed. Witnesses signing a Will can be a spouse or family, can be named executor or guardian, and can be getting Will gifts, but it is a bit better if people without these connections are used as witnesses.

FORM 1:
LAST WILL AND TESTAMENT (WITH GUARDIANS)

LAST WILL AND TESTAMENT

I, _____, a resident of _____ County, Pennsylvania, hereby make, publish, and declare this as my Last Will and Testament (called here my "Will"), and I hereby revoke any Wills and Codicils earlier made by me.

1. GIFTS. I give the following gifts which are specific gifts except any gifts of money amounts are general gifts.

I give _____

to _____ if they survive me.

I give _____

to _____ if they survive me.

I give _____

to _____ if they survive me.

I give _____

to _____ if they survive me.

I give _____

to _____ if they survive me.

I give _____

to _____ if they survive me.

2. TANGIBLE PERSONAL PROPERTY WRITINGS. I may leave signed writings giving tangible personal property, and I direct all such writings and gifts in them be incorporated by reference into this Will or treated as legally binding by other means including because they are made with testamentary intent. But if property is specifically given in this Will a contrary gift in such writings has no effect. Any such writings are not revoked by this Will. Any such writings and gifts in them not found by 60 days after my death shall have no effect. A recipient getting property in such writings must survive me by 60 days for a gift to them to have any effect. Several such writings are intended as and should be construed as a single document to all be followed. If the same property is given in multiple writings the more recently done page shall control.

3. RESIDUE. I give all my property and estate remaining and not given or used by other Will provisions or other ways, whether now owned or later acquired, wherever located, and of any kind and nature including personal, real, and mixed property, including the rest, residue, and remainder of my estate (all of which is called in this Will the "residue"), as follows: to _____
if they survive me, but if they all do not survive me I give the just described property to
_____ or their lineal descendants per stirpes.
Part of this residue section may be left unfilled, and any used part should be given effect.

4. ADMINISTRATION. I name and appoint _____ as executor of my Will and my estate.

5. GUARDIANS. If any of my children have not reached age 18 I name and appoint
_____ to be guardian of the person of such children.
I also name and appoint _____ as guardian of the estate for such children and their estate and property, and also for any other persons under age 18 who receive or possess property and their estate and property.

6. MISCELLANEOUS. The following applies to this Will and generally.
   I request unsupervised and informal administration and probate of my estate and Will.
   Plural, singular, or gender meanings do not limit any Will part, such as use of "they".
   Any executor or guardian of any type acting under this Will or otherwise shall serve without bond, surety, or other security including for performance of their duties.
   An executor shall sell a gift unless all beneficiaries getting it agree on its use or sale.
   No unfilled Will part is a mistake, and Will parts about the residue may be left blank.
   The priority of Will gifts of the same type is based on the order they appear.
   The words "give" and "gift" mean the same as devise, bequest, grant, legacy or similar.
   The words "survive" or "surviving" in a gift or other place creates an absolute condition that must be met or a gift fails and anti-lapse laws or similar have no effect.
   Any person or entity not surviving me by 60 days shall be deemed to not survive me.
   For gifts to multiple beneficiaries a non-surviving beneficiary's share goes to other beneficiaries in proportion to shares they are taking, including for the residue or if a gift requires or mentions survival, but not if an alternate beneficiary is provided in the Will.
   Any executor and guardian of any type is given as much power, authority, and discretion that may be given by law, including power to (with no liability for change in

value) sell, lease, assign, mortgage, invest, operate, hold, exchange, and transfer in any way any property including of the estate, settle claims for and against the estate or any person, do any tax action or filing, and have power of sale for real property, all with no need for act of any court or party, and all with no need for any filing or inventory.

Any executor has power to take any action involving an ancillary estate, give different kinds, portions or undivided interests in property to beneficiaries and assign value to all things, and do any distribution or division of my estate or property in cash or in kind.

Any executor may any time and in any amount pay debts of mine or my estate they in their sole and absolute discretion finds are valid, enforceable, timely, and fair, including of a last illness, for funeral and related things, with no filing or act of court or other party.

For property or other thing going to minors an executor without act of court has power to transfer property to: the minor, any adult the minor lives with, a guardian of the estate named by Will or a court, or a custodian under the Pennsylvania Uniform Transfers to Minors Act or similar law. For such minors the person named guardian of the estate in this Will is nominated and named as custodian under the Pennsylvania Uniform Transfers to Minors Act or similar law, or if needed any executor may name a custodian.

Any successor including of an executor or guardian of any type named in this Will shall have all powers, privileges, immunities and exemptions their predecessor had.

My not giving more to children and other family is intentional and not a mistake.

Residue includes lapsed or failed gifts, insurance paid to the estate, inheritances owed testator, and property testator had power of appointment or testamentary disposition over.

TESTATOR

I have signed this my Last Will and Testament this __ day of _____, 20__.

_____
Testator

WITNESSES

Signed by _____, the Testator, as the Last Will and Testament of Testator, in the presence of both of us, who, at Testator's request and in Testator's presence and the presence of each other, have signed our names as witnesses.

_____	_____
Witness	Address
_____	_____
Witness	Address

CHAPTER 5
FORM 2: LAST WILL AND TESTAMENT (NO GUARDIANS)

FORM 2 IS A WILL WITH NO GUARDIANS PARAGRAPH

Form 2 is just like the Will in Form 1 and is flexible and lets people gift their property and money most ways. But Form 2 unlike Form 1 has no "Guardians" paragraph and is a Will for a person without a child under 18 and not giving anything to any minors under 18.

WILL IN FORM 2 HAS BASIC LAYOUT WITH SEVERAL PARTS TO FILL OUT

The Will in Form 2 has a basic layout with several parts for a person to fill out to use.

At its start the Will has a place for a person making the Will to put their full legal name and county.

The 1st paragraph, "Gifts", has many spaces for a person to a) make specific gifts by a person describing particular property and naming persons to get these things, and b) make money gifts by a person writing in money amounts and naming persons to get this money.

The 2nd paragraph, "Tangible Personal Property List", just says to follow any gift lists people write.

The 3rd paragraph, "Residue", gives any property and money not used by other parts of the Will or in other ways, which is done by writing here the names of persons to get this.

The 4th paragraph, "Administration", has a space to write in someone's name to be "executor" to if needed handle most matters after a person's death, and often named is a spouse, child, or friend.

The Will in Form 2 has no "Guardians" paragraph unlike the Will in Form 1.

The 5th paragraph, "Miscellaneous", just has many sentences of legal language that help avoid certain legal problems and help explain the Will.

Last is where the Will maker signs their full name and 2 witnesses sign and write their addresses.

As just explained, the Will parts let people gift specific property and money, say any gift lists should be followed, gift the residue, name an executor, name guardians, and sign the end to make it valid.

RESIDUE CLAUSE HAS 2 PLACES TO NAME PEOPLE TO GET ANYTHING LEFT

In a Will's "residue clause" anything not used by other parts of the Will or other means is gifted to the persons named in the residue clause. A residue clause is a "catch-all" making sure all property and money goes to someone, or many people use the residue clause to gift most of their things. The residue clause in this book's Wills is written to have:

1) a 1st space to name 1 or more persons to get the residue (but anyone named here must
    survive to get things or their share goes to others named here), and

2) a 2nd space to name people to get things if all in the 1st space don't survive (any named
    here who don't survive have their share go to descendants due to language used in the Will).

Most people name in the 1st space a spouse or closest family and in the 2nd space name their next closest family or friends. Helpful special options exist which many people can use:

a) People can in the residue clause leave the 1st space empty and only name people in the
    2nd space to ensure if someone named dies their descendants get their share;

b) People can repeat names in the 2 clause spaces if there is only 1 person or group to target; and

c) People can in either of the residue clause's spaces gift using percentages.

This may seem complex but whoever is named in the 1st used space gets things if they survive.

WILL IS DONE BY PERSON SIGNING BEFORE 2 WITNESSES WHO SIGN TOO

A Will to be completed should be signed by the person doing the Will before 2 witnesses who then sign too. Everyone signing should be present and watch others sign. It is optional but before signing some people doing a Will hold it up and say to witnesses things like, "This is the Will I want and want you to witness". Before signing most witnesses read quietly to themselves the paragraph they sign, and witnesses need not read or have read to them the entire Will. In paragraphs that are signed there are places to add some names and dates, and this can be done by the person signing or beforehand by anyone. Last is a spot for witnesses to write their addresses just in case needed later. Witnesses should be at least 18 but if possible young enough to be available later if needed. Witnesses signing a Will can be a spouse or family, can be named executor or guardian, and can be getting Will gifts, but it is a bit better if people without these connections are used as witnesses.

FORM 2:
LAST WILL AND TESTAMENT (NO GUARDIANS)

LAST WILL AND TESTAMENT

I, _____, a resident of _____ County, Pennsylvania, hereby make, publish, and declare this as my Last Will and Testament (called here my "Will"), and I hereby revoke any Wills and Codicils earlier made by me.

1. GIFTS. I give the following gifts which are specific gifts except any gifts of money amounts are general gifts.

I give _____
to _____ if they survive me.

I give _____
to _____ if they survive me.

I give _____
to _____ if they survive me.

I give _____
to _____ if they survive me.

I give _____
to _____ if they survive me.

I give _____
to _____ if they survive me.

2. TANGIBLE PERSONAL PROPERTY WRITINGS. I may leave signed writings giving tangible personal property, and I direct all such writings and gifts in them be incorporated by reference into this Will or treated as legally binding by other means including because they are made with testamentary intent. But if property is specifically given in this Will a contrary gift in such writings has no effect. Any such writings are not revoked by this Will. Any such writings and gifts in them not found by 60 days after my death shall have no effect. A recipient getting property in such writings must survive me by 60 days for a gift to them to have any effect. Several such writings are intended as and should be construed as a single document to all be followed. If the same property is given in multiple writings the more recently done page shall control.

3. RESIDUE. I give all my property and estate remaining and not given or used by other Will provisions or other ways, whether now owned or later acquired, wherever located, and of any kind and nature including personal, real, and mixed property, including the rest, residue, and remainder of my estate (all of which is called in this Will the "residue"), as follows: to _____
if they survive me, but if they all do not survive me I give the just described property to
_____ or their lineal descendants per stirpes.
Part of this residue section may be left unfilled, and any used part should be given effect.

4. ADMINISTRATION. I name and appoint _____ as executor of my Will and my estate.

5. MISCELLANEOUS. The following applies to this Will and generally.

I request unsupervised and informal administration and probate of my estate and Will.

Plural, singular, or gender meanings do not limit any Will part, such as use of "they".

Any executor or guardian of any type acting under this Will or otherwise shall serve without bond, surety, or other security including for performance of their duties.

An executor shall sell a gift unless all beneficiaries getting it agree on its use or sale.

No unfilled Will part is a mistake, and Will parts about the residue may be left blank.

The priority of Will gifts of the same type is based on the order they appear.

The words "give" and "gift" mean the same as devise, bequest, grant, legacy or similar.

The words "survive" or "surviving" in a gift or other place creates an absolute condition that must be met or a gift fails and anti-lapse laws or similar have no effect.

Any person or entity not surviving me by 60 days shall be deemed to not survive me.

For gifts to multiple beneficiaries a non-surviving beneficiary's share goes to other beneficiaries in proportion to shares they are taking, including for the residue or if a gift requires or mentions survival, but not if an alternate beneficiary is provided in the Will.

Any executor and guardian of any type is given as much power, authority, and discretion that may be given by law, including power to (with no liability for change in value) sell, lease, assign, mortgage, invest, operate, hold, exchange, and transfer in any way any property including of the estate, settle claims for and against the estate or any person, do any tax action or filing, and have power of sale for real property, all with no need for act of any court or party, and all with no need for any filing or inventory.

Any executor has power to take any action involving an ancillary estate, give different kinds, portions or undivided interests in property to beneficiaries and assign value to all things, and do any distribution or division of my estate or property in cash or in kind.

Any executor may any time and in any amount pay debts of mine or my estate they in their sole and absolute discretion finds are valid, enforceable, timely, and fair, including of a last illness, for funeral and related things, with no filing or act of court or other party.

For property or other thing going to minors an executor without act of court has power to transfer property to: the minor, any adult the minor lives with, a guardian of the estate named by Will or a court, or a custodian under the Pennsylvania Uniform Transfers to Minors Act or similar law. For such minors the person named guardian of the estate in this Will is nominated and named as custodian under the Pennsylvania Uniform Transfers to Minors Act or similar law, or if needed any executor may name a custodian.

Any successor including of an executor or guardian of any type named in this Will shall have all powers, privileges, immunities and exemptions their predecessor had.

My not giving more to children and other family is intentional and not a mistake.

Residue includes lapsed or failed gifts, insurance paid to the estate, inheritances owed testator, and property testator had power of appointment or testamentary disposition over.

TESTATOR

I have signed this my Last Will and Testament this __ day of _____, 20__.

_____
Testator

WITNESSES

Signed by _____, the Testator, as the Last Will and Testament of Testator, in the presence of both of us, who, at Testator's request and in Testator's presence and the presence of each other, have signed our names as witnesses.

_____   _____
Witness   Address

_____   _____
Witness   Address

CHAPTER 6
FORM 3: SELF-PROVING AFFIDAVIT

FORM 3 IS DONE WITH A WILL TO SUPPORT A WILL AND AVOID LATER WORK

The "Self-Proving Affidavit" form is a standard form by the state legislature and found in law at 20 Pa. C. S. § 3132.1. This form reduces later legal work and makes the Will more likely to be followed.

DOING SELF-PROVING AFFIDAVIT WITH WILL IS OPTIONAL BUT COMMON

This form is optional but is often done when a Will is signed or anytime later to help with legal work done after the person who made the Will dies. If this form is not done witnesses to a Will signing may have to be found after a death and testify convincingly in court that the Will was signed correctly (or in some cases other evidence can be used). Also, if this form is done it is more likely a Will can be sufficiently proven so is followed. Usually a Self-Proving Affidavit form is signed minutes after a Will is signed, or the form can be done anytime later when people are before a notary.

DO FORM BY PERSON DOING WILL AND WITNESSES SIGNING BEFORE NOTARY

The Self-Proving Affidavit form must be signed by the person who did the Will and 2 witnesses to the Will signing while everyone is before a notary. Normally this is all done by people together, but the law does say people can sign 2 or 3 separate copies of the form when before a notary if they are not all together but this is not recommended. A notary can be found at some banks, insurance agencies, courts, copy places, government offices, business offices, or by hiring a notary from a phonebook (this option can avoid problems but may require buying other services). A lawyer not a notary can also be used to complete this form but this is less common and this book's form has had the words for this option removed. When done a Self-Proving Affidavit form should be attached by paperclip or staple to the Will it supports.

FORM 3:
SELF-PROVING AFFIDAVIT

SELF-PROVING AFFIDAVIT

Acknowledgment

Commonwealth of Pennsylvania

County of _____

I, _____, the testator whose name is signed to the attached or foregoing instrument, having been duly qualified according to law, do hereby acknowledge that I signed and executed the instrument as my Last Will; and that I signed it willingly and as my free and voluntary act for the purposes therein expressed.

Sworn to or affirmed and acknowledged before me by _____, the testator, this ___ day of _____, 20___.

_____
(Testator)

_____
(Signature of officer)

(Seal and official capacity of officer)

Affidavit

Commonwealth of Pennsylvania

County of _____

We, _____ and _____, the witnesses whose names are signed to the attached or foregoing instrument, being duly qualified according to law, do depose and say that we were present and saw the testator sign and execute the instrument as his Last Will; that the testator signed willingly and executed it as his free and voluntary act for the purposes therein expressed; that each subscribing witness in the hearing and sight of the testator signed the will as a witness; and that to the best of our knowledge the testator was at that time 18 or more years of age, of sound mind and under no constraint or undue influence.

Sworn to or affirmed and subscribed to before me by _____ and _____, witnesses, this ___ day of _____, 20___.

_____
Witness

_____
Witness

_____
(Signature of officer)

(Seal and official capacity of officer)

CHAPTER 7
FORM 4: TANGIBLE PERSONAL PROPERTY LIST

FORM LETS GIFTS OF NORMAL PROPERTY BE WRITTEN OUTSIDE A WILL

Form 4 the "Tangible Personal Property List" form (often called a "Gift Memorandum") lets people write down wanted gifts of tangible personal property they want to occur after their death.

PEOPLE CAN WRITE IN LISTS WANTED GIFTS

A person in a list can write down gifts they wants to happen after their death. By law a Will can "incorporate by reference" and enforce any such writings people did on an earlier date than the Will. Legally lists done after a Will might not be binding despite some state law saying any writing can add to or be a Will if signed, so a person may want to do things so lists appear dated earlier than a Will. But no matter what the law says usually family and friends will follow lists or other writings a person did. Using lists is suggested in newspapers and by lawyers. People can do many lists but it is better to do 1 big list stapled together and signed on 1 date. It is recommended people do not put valuable property in lists.

LISTS ONLY GIVES "TANGIBLE PERSONAL PROPERTY" NOT GIVEN IN WILL

This book's form only gives "tangible personal property", so only "tangible" property with solid form (not accounts or most investments), only "personal property" so not real property (not buildings or land), and not money (so not coins or paper money even if antiques). Property used in a trade or business usually should not be in a list. Valuable property should not given in a list. Lists most often are used to gift furniture, clothing, appliances, tools, and jewelry. If a Will specifically gives an item usually the Will is followed over anything said in a list. A list needs enough detail so people who knew a decedent can tell the likely meaning. This book's form does say if a person has not lived past the Will maker by 60 days then a list gift to them has no effect, and also says lists not found by 60 days after a person's death will not be followed. Examples of list gifts are: "Silver Lamp to Amy Smith", "Small blue diamond ring to Kay Coe", and "Winter coats and boats to Mary Sue Paulson".

TANGIBLE PERSONAL PROPERTY LIST MUST BE SIGNED AND DATED

To be completed a Tangible Personal Property List form should be signed and dated. To be followed a list must be found after a person's death, and lists are often paperclipped to a Will or kept nearby. A list can be revoked by writing canceled on it, destroying it, or just having it so it is not found after a person's death to be followed.

FORM 4:
TANGIBLE PERSONAL PROPERTY LIST

TANGIBLE PERSONAL PROPERTY LIST

I declare this writing makes gifts of tangible personal property to occur at my death and is made with testamentary intent. I make the gifts below but only if a recipient survives me by 60 days and if they do not then the gift to them shall have no effect. This list and gifts in it if not found by 60 days after my death shall have no effect. If property is specifically given in a Will a gift of such property here has no effect.

PROPERTY ITEMS GIFTED   **NAMES OF RECIPIENTS**

_____   _____

_____   _____

_____   _____

_____   _____

_____   _____

_____   _____

_____   _____

_____   _____

_____   _____

_____   _____

_____   _____

_____   _____

_____   _____

DATE: _____   **SIGNED:** _____

CHAPTER 8
FORM 5: CODICIL

FORM 5 "CODICIL" FORM CAN BE USED TO CHANGE PARTS OF A WILL

To change parts of an existing Will it is usually best to do a new Will to reduce the chance of confusion about what words are meant. But if wanted one can use a "Codicil" form to change parts of a Will, to add to a Will, or to remove parts of a Will.

IN CODICIL TO CHANGE WILL JUST LIST WORDS TO REMOVE AND TO ADD

In a Codicil form usually one first writes the words to be removed from a Will, then one writes the new words to be added to a Will. Or the Codicil can be used to add whole new things or remove things. Often the Codicil does simple things that should not be too confusing to others like replacing a beneficiary name, replacing property in a gift, adding or deleting a whole gift, or naming a different person as executor or guardian. These things might be done because people named in a Will have died or no longer need things, or because gifted property in a Will is no longer owned so needs to be replaced.

CODICIL MUST BE SIGNED BEFORE 2 WITNESSES WHO SIGN

To be valid a Codicil must be signed just like a Will and meet all the normal requirements for a Will signing. Basically, the person making the document must sign before 2 witnesses who also sign. Under Pennsylvania law the witnesses can be a spouse or family, or persons getting gifts in the Will or Codicil, or persons named as executor or guardian, but using people without these links as witnesses is better. When completed a Codicil document should be kept so it is found with the Will it modifies.

FORM 5:
CODICIL

CODICIL

I, _____, a resident of _____ County, Pennsylvania, declare this to be a Codicil to my Will dated _____.

FIRST: I hereby do revoke the part of my Will that reads as follows:

_____

_____

_____.

SECOND: I hereby do add the following part to my Will:

_____

_____

_____.

THIRD: In all other respects I do confirm and republish the above-described Will.

TESTATOR

I, the Testator, sign, publish, and declare I sign and execute this document as my Codicil, that I sign it willingly as a free and voluntary act for the purposes expressed therein, and that I am at least 18 years of age and of sound mind and under no constraint or undue influence, this ___ day of _____, 20___.

_____
Testator

WITNESSES

We, the undersigned, declare in our presence the foregoing document was willingly published, declared, and signed by the above-named Testator as his or her Codicil, that to the best of our knowledge the Testator is at least 18 years of age and of sound mind and under no constraint or undue influence, that each of us is at least 18 years old, and that in the presence and hearing of Testator and each other we sign our names as witnesses.

_____   _____
Witness   Address

_____   _____
Witness   Address

CHAPTER 9
FORM 6: DURABLE HEALTH CARE POWER OF ATTORNEY AND HEALTH CARE TREATMENT INSTRUCTIONS (LIVING WILL)

FORM LETS PERSON NAME HEALTH CARE AGENT AND GIVE INSTRUCTIONS

In case a person later can't control their health care this form lets someone be named "Health Care Agent" to control health care, and also lets health care instructions be given. This is a standard form by the state legislature and is found in law at 20 Pa. C. S. § 5471, and is often called an "Advance Directive" for short. It is sometimes called a "Living Will" since it is a Will taking effect during life. This new form is meant to replace several smaller old documents.

CAN NAME SOMEONE "HEALTH CARE AGENT" IN CASE EVER NEEDED

In the "Durable Health Care Power of Attorney" part of the form someone at least 18 can be named "Health Care Agent" to control health care if doctors fine a person is incapacitated (can't control things due to inability to communicate, inability to reason or stay conscious, or similar). Without a form if needed the law gives power over health care to (in order) a spouse, child, parents, and other family, but naming a spouse or child as Agent in a form can save time and legal work. Agents must serve "best interests" of a person, but must follow written or verbal orders a person gives them. An Agent or family in charge may see medical records. "Durable" means still effective if someone is incapacitated.

CAN GIVE INSTRUCTIONS ABOUT HEALTH CARE IN CASE EVER NEEDED

In the "Treatment Instructions" part and other parts of the form in case ever needed a person can give health care instructions for their Agent, doctors, and family to follow. Importantly, many people skip most instructions since they trust the Agent and it is hard to predict things. The part of the form or similar forms with instructions is called a "Living Will" since it is like a Will that takes effect during life.

DO FORM BY PERSON SIGNING BEFORE 2 WITNESSES WHO ALSO SIGN

The form to be valid is signed by the person doing the form before 2 witnesses who then sign too. Witnesses must be at least 18 and not working for any health care provider giving care, and witnesses can be anyone named Agent in the form. There is a place for a notary but this is not required, and this can be left blank or removed from a form if wanted. When the form is signed usually the named Agent is given the original to use, and copies are shown to health care providers. The form can be revoked by verbally or in writing telling an Agent and then telling others who might keep relying on the form.

FORM 6:
DURABLE HEALTH CARE POWER OF ATTORNEY AND HEALTH CARE TREATMENT INSTRUCTIONS (LIVING WILL)

DURABLE HEALTH CARE POWER OF ATTORNEY AND HEALTH CARE TREATMENT INSTRUCTIONS (LIVING WILL)

PART I
INTRODUCTORY REMARKS ON
HEALTH CARE DECISION MAKING

You have the right to decide the type of health care you want.

Should you become unable to understand, make or communicate decisions about medical care, your wishes for medical treatment are most likely to be followed if you express those wishes in advance by:

(1) naming a health care agent to decide treatment for you; and

(2) giving health care treatment instructions to your health care agent or health care provider.

An advance health care directive is a written set of instructions expressing your wishes for medical treatment. It may contain a health care power of attorney, where you name a person called a "health care agent" to decide treatment for you, and a living will, where you tell your health care agent and health care providers your choices regarding the initiation, continuation, withholding or withdrawal of life-sustaining treatment and other specific directions.

You may limit your health care agent's involvement in deciding your medical treatment so that your health care agent will speak for you only when you are unable to speak for yourself or you may give your health care agent the power to speak for you immediately. This combined form gives your health care agent the power to speak for you only when you are unable to speak for yourself. A living will cannot be followed unless your attending physician determines that you lack the ability to understand, make or communicate health care decisions for yourself, and you are either permanently unconscious or you have an end-stage medical condition, which is a condition that will result in death despite the introduction or continuation of medical treatment. You, and not your health care agent, remain responsible for the cost of your medical care.

If you do not write down your wishes about your health care in advance, and if later you become unable to understand, make or communicate these decisions, those wishes may not be honored because they may remain unknown to others.

A health care provider who refuses to honor your wishes about health care must tell you of its refusal and help to transfer you to a health care provider who will honor your wishes.

You should give a copy of your advance health care directive (a living will, health care power of attorney or a document containing both) to your health care agent, your physicians, family members and others whom you expect would likely attend to your needs if you become unable to understand, make or communicate decisions about medical care. If your health care wishes change, tell your physician and write a new advance health care directive to replace your old one. It is important in selecting a health care agent that you choose a person you trust who is likely to be available in a medical situation where you cannot make decisions for yourself. You should inform that person that you have appointed him or her as your health care agent and discuss your beliefs and values with him or her so that your health care agent will understand your health care objectives.

You may wish to consult with knowledgeable, trusted individuals such as family members, your physician or clergy when considering an expression of your values and health care wishes. You are free to create your own advance health care directive to convey your wishes regarding medical treatment. The following form is an example of an advance health care directive that combines a health care power of attorney with a living will.

NOTES ABOUT THE USE OF THIS FORM

If you decide to use this form or create your own advance health care directive, you should consult with your physician and your attorney to make sure that your wishes are clearly expressed and comply with the law.

If you decide to use this form but disagree with any of its statements, you may cross out those statements.

You may add comments to this form or use your own form to help your physician or health care agent decide your medical care.

This form is designed to give your health care agent broad powers to make health care decisions for you whenever you cannot make them for yourself. It is also designed to express a desire to limit or authorize care if you have an end-stage medical condition or are permanently unconscious. If you do not desire to give your health care agent broad powers, or you do not wish to limit your care if you have an end-stage medical condition or are permanently unconscious, you may wish to use a different form or create your own. YOU SHOULD ALSO USE A DIFFERENT FORM IF YOU WISH TO EXPRESS YOUR PREFERENCES IN MORE DETAIL THAN THIS FORM ALLOWS OR IF YOU WISH FOR YOUR HEALTH CARE AGENT TO BE ABLE TO SPEAK FOR YOU IMMEDIATELY. In these situations, it is particularly important that you consult with your attorney and physician to make sure that your wishes are clearly expressed.

This form allows you to tell your health care agent your goals if you have an end-stage medical condition or other extreme and irreversible medical condition, such as advanced Alzheimer's disease. Do you want medical care applied aggressively in these situations or would you consider such aggressive medical care burdensome and undesirable?

You may choose whether you want your health care agent to be bound by your instructions or whether you want you health care agent to be able to decide at the time what course of treatment the health care agent thinks most fully reflects your wishes and values.

If you are a woman and diagnosed as being pregnant at the time a health care decision would otherwise be made pursuant to this form, the laws of this Commonwealth prohibit implementation of that decision if it directs that life-sustaining treatment, including nutrition and hydration, be withheld or withdrawn from you, unless your attending physician and an obstetrician who have examined you certify in your medical record that the life-sustaining treatments:

(1) will not maintain you in such a way as to permit the continuing development and live birth of the unborn child;

(2) will be physically harmful to you; or

(3) will cause pain to you that cannot be alleviated by medication.

A physician is not required to perform a pregnancy test on you unless the physician has reason to believe that you may be pregnant.

Pennsylvania law protects your health care agent and health care providers from any legal liability for following in good faith your wishes as expressed in the form or by your health care agent's direction. It does not otherwise change professional standards or excuse negligence in the way your wishes are carried out. If you have any questions about the law, consult an attorney for guidance.

This form and explanation is not intended to take the place of specific legal or medical advice for which you should rely upon your own attorney and physician.

PART II
DURABLE HEALTH CARE POWER OF ATTORNEY

I _____, of _____ County, Pennsylvania, appoint the person named below to be my health care agent to make health and personal care decisions for me.

Effective immediately and continuously until my death or revocation by a writing signed by me or someone authorized to make health care treatment decisions for me, I authorize all health care providers or other covered entities to disclose to my health care agent, upon my agent's request, any information, oral or written, regarding my physical or mental health, including, but not limited to, medical and hospital records and what is otherwise private, privileged, protected or personal health information, such as health information as defined and described in the Health Insurance Portability and Accountability Act of 1996 (Public Law 104—191, 110 Stat. 1936), the regulations promulgated thereunder and any other State or local laws and rules. Information disclosed by a health care provider or other covered entity may be redisclosed and may no longer be subject to the privacy rules provided by 45 C.F.R. Pt. 164.

The remainder of this document will take effect when and only when I lack the ability to understand, make or communicate a choice regarding a health or personal care decision as verified by my attending physician. My health care agent may not delegate the authority to make decisions.

MY HEALTH CARE AGENT HAS ALL OF THE FOLLOWING POWERS SUBJECT TO THE HEALTH CARE TREATMENT INSTRUCTIONS THAT FOLLOW IN PART III (CROSS OUT ANY POWERS YOU DO NOT WANT TO GIVE YOUR HEALTH CARE AGENT):

1. To authorize, withhold or withdraw medical care and surgical procedures.

2. To authorize, withhold or withdraw nutrition (food) or hydration (water) medically supplied by tube through my nose, stomach, intestines, arteries or veins.

3. To authorize my admission to or discharge from a medical, nursing, residential or similar facility and to make agreements for my care and health insurance for my care, including hospice and/or palliative care.

4. To hire and fire medical, social service and other support personnel responsible for my care.

5. To take any legal action necessary to do what I have directed.

6. To request that a physician responsible for my care issue a do-not-resuscitate (DNR) order, including an out-of-hospital DNR order, and sign any required documents   and consents.

APPOINTMENT OF HEALTH CARE AGENT

I appoint the following health care agent:

Health Care Agent: _____ (Name and relationship)

Address: _____

_____

Telephone Number: Home _____ Work _____

E-Mail: _____

IF YOU DO NOT NAME A HEALTH CARE AGENT, HEALTH CARE PROVIDERS WILL ASK YOUR FAMILY OR AN ADULT WHO KNOWS YOUR PREFERENCES AND VALUES FOR HELP IN DETERMINING YOUR WISHES FOR TREATMENT. NOTE THAT YOU MAY NOT APPOINT YOUR DOCTOR OR OTHER HEALTH CARE PROVIDER AS YOUR HEALTH CARE AGENT UNLESS RELATED TO YOU BY BLOOD, MARRIAGE OR ADOPTION.

If my health care agent is not readily available or if my health care agent is my spouse and an action for divorce is filed by either of us after the date of this document, I appoint the person or persons named below in the order named. (It is helpful, but not required, to name alternative health care agents.)

First Alternative Health Care Agent: _____ (Name and relationship)

Address: _____

_____

Telephone Number: Home _____ Work _____

E-Mail: _____

Second Alternative Health Care Agent: _____ (Name and relationship)

Address: _____

_____

Telephone Number: Home _____ Work _____

E-Mail: _____

GUIDANCE FOR HEALTH CARE AGENT (OPTIONAL)

GOALS

If I have an end-stage medical condition or other extreme irreversible medical condition, my goals in making medical decisions are as follows (insert your personal priorities such as comfort, care, preservation of mental function, etc.): _____

_____

_____

_____

_____

_____

_____

_____

_____

_____

_____

SEVERE BRAIN DAMAGE OR BRAIN DISEASE

If I should suffer from severe and irreversible brain damage or brain disease with no realistic hope of significant recovery, I would consider such a condition intolerable and the application of aggressive medical care to be burdensome. I therefore request that my health care agent respond to any intervening (other and separate) life-threatening conditions in the same manner as directed for an end-stage medical condition or state of permanent unconsciousness as I have indicated below.

Initials _____ I agree

Initials _____ I disagree

PART III

HEALTH CARE TREATMENT INSTRUCTIONS IN THE EVENT OF END-STAGE MEDICAL CONDITION OR PERMANENT UNCONSCIOUSNESS (LIVING WILL)

The following health care treatment instructions exercise my right to make my own health care decisions. These instructions are intended to provide clear and convincing evidence of my wishes to be followed when I lack the capacity to understand, make or communicate my treatment decisions:

IF I HAVE AN END-STAGE MEDICAL CONDITION (WHICH WILL RESULT IN MY DEATH, DESPITE THE INTRODUCTION OR CONTINUATION OF MEDICAL TREATMENT) OR AM PERMANENTLY UNCONSCIOUS SUCH AS AN IRREVERSIBLE COMA OR AN IRREVERSIBLE VEGETATIVE STATE AND THERE IS NO REALISTIC HOPE OF SIGNIFICANT RECOVERY, ALL OF THE FOLLOWING APPLY (CROSS OUT ANY TREATMENT INSTRUCTIONS WITH WHICH YOU DO NOT AGREE):

1. I direct that I be given health care treatment to relieve pain or provide comfort even if such treatment might shorten my life, suppress my appetite or my breathing, or be habit forming.

2. I direct that all life-prolonging procedures be withheld or withdrawn.

3. I specifically do not want any of the following as life prolonging procedures: (If you wish to receive any of these treatments, write "I do want" after the treatment)

heart-lung resuscitation (CPR) _____

mechanical ventilator (breathing machine) _____

dialysis (kidney machine) _____

surgery _____

chemotherapy _____

radiation treatment _____

antibiotics _____

Please indicate whether you want nutrition (food) or hydration (water) medically supplied by a tube into your nose, stomach, intestine, arteries, or veins if you have an end-stage medical condition or are permanently unconscious and there is no realistic hope of significant recovery.

(Initial only one statement).

TUBE FEEDINGS

_____ I want tube feedings to be given

OR

NO TUBE FEEDINGS

_____ I do not want tube feedings to be given.

HEALTH CARE AGENT'S USE OF INSTRUCTIONS
(INITIAL ONE OPTION ONLY)

_____ My health care agent must follow these instructions.

OR

_____ These instructions are only guidance. My health care agent shall have final say and may override any of my instructions. (Indicate any exceptions)_____

_____

_____

_____

_____

If I did not appoint a health care agent, these instructions shall be followed.

LEGAL PROTECTION

Pennsylvania law protects my health care agent and health care providers from any legal liability for their good faith actions in following my wishes as expressed in this form or in complying with my health care agent's direction. On behalf of myself, my executors and heirs, I further hold my health care agent and my health care providers harmless and indemnify them against any claim for their good faith actions in recognizing my health care agent's authority or in following my treatment instructions.

ORGAN DONATION
(INITIAL ONE OPTION ONLY)

_____ I consent to donate my organs and tissues at the time of my death for the purpose of transplant, medical study or education. (Insert any limitations you desire on donation of specific organs or tissues or uses for donation of organs and tissues.) _____

OR

_____ I do not consent to donate my organs or tissues at the time of my death.

SIGNATURE

Having carefully read this document, I have signed it this ___ day of_____, 20___, revoking all previous health care powers of attorney and health care treatment instructions.

_____
(SIGN FULL NAME HERE FOR HEALTH CARE POWER OF ATTORNEY AND HEALTH CARE TREATMENT INSTRUCTIONS.)

WITNESS: _____

WITNESS: _____

Two witnesses at least 18 years of age are required by Pennsylvania law and should witness your signature in each other's presence. A person who signs this document on behalf of and at the direction of a principal may not be a witness. (It is preferable if the witnesses are not your heirs, nor your creditors, nor employed by any of your health care providers.)

NOTARIZATION (OPTIONAL)

(Notarization of document is not required by Pennsylvania law, but if the document is both witnessed and notarized, it is more likely to be honored by the laws of some other states.)

On this ___ day of_____, 20___, before me personally appeared the aforesaid declarant and principal, to me known to be the person described in and who executed the foregoing instrument and acknowledged that he/she executed the same as his/her free act and deed.

IN WITNESS WHEREOF, I have hereunto set my hand and affixed my official seal in the County of _____, State of _____ the day and year first above written.

_____
Notary Public

_____
My commission expires

CHAPTER 10
FORM 7: P.O.L.S.T. (DO NOT RESUSCITATE)

FORM LETS PEOPLE SAY CERTAIN EMERGENCY CARE IS NOT TO BE GIVEN

Form 7 is the P.O.L.S.T. form , short for "Pennsylvania Orders For Life-Sustaining Treatment". This form is often called a "Do Not Resuscitate" (this is an older form that is being replaced). The form lets people say some emergency care is not to be given. The general goal of the form is to avoid care likely to do little long-term good and is difficult or costly to endure, and to avoid care that blocks a death that is more natural and easier. This is a standard form by the Department of Health.

FORM ORDERS PARAMEDICS AND OTHERS NOT TO TRY C.P.R. AND SIMILAR

People in very bad health can ask for a P.O.L.S.T. form to quickly show paramedics and other medical personnel no C.P.R. and some other major actions listed should not be tried. Doctors must sign the form and may delay doing a P.O.L.S.T. form if a person is not in extreme poor health. The form has spots to cover C.P.R. (cardiopulmonary resuscitation to try restarting a heart and breathing), antibiotics, artificial food or water (forced by tube), and any other care that is written in. Older "Do Not Resuscitate Order" forms covers only C.P.R. Paramedics and others in a hurry usually only look for and follow P.O.L.S.T. or Do Not Resuscitate Order forms and ignore other forms. The P.O.L.S.T. is most y used if people are at home, with family, or traveling. In a hospital, nursing home, or similar usually people give instructions to doctors or fill out hospital forms (or forms like th's book's Form 5).

KEEP FORM NEAR BODY TO BE FOLLOWED BUT IT CAN BE REVOKED

To make sure a form is followed people should keep it near or on their body, or some people wear a special "bracelet" showing the form details. By law comfort care and pain relief is always given, so even with a form people often call for paramedics or other help. A person is usually free to verbally or in writing revoke the form anytime (like ask for C.P.R. from paramedics). As part of revocation any places that saw a form should be told or they may continue to follow the form.

FORM IS COMPLETED BY DOCTOR AND PERSON SIGNING

The P.O.L.S.T. form is completed by the person doing the form signing and also a doctor or similar signing. A doctor usually provides this form and explains the options. If a person is incapacitated another person with power to control health care can request a form and sign, but only if this matches known wishes of a person. Once signed usually a person keeps the original form on or near their body to be seen (or they wear a special bracelet), and a copy is given to all places that may give care.

FORM 7:
P.O.L.S.T. (DO NOT RESUSCITATE)

pennsylvania
DEPARTMENT OF HEALTH

Pennsylvania
Orders for Life-Sustaining
Treatment (POLST)

Last Name

First/Middle Initial

Date of Birth

FIRST follow these orders, **THEN** contact physician, certified registered nurse practitioner or physician assistant. This is an Order Sheet based on the person's medical condition and wishes at the time the orders were issued. Everyone shall be treated with dignity and respect.

A Check One	**CARDIOPULMONARY RESUSCITATION (CPR): Person has no pulse <u>and</u> is not breathing.** ☐ CPR/Attempt Resuscitation ☐ DNR/Do Not Attempt Resuscitation (Allow Natural Death) When not in cardiopulmonary arrest, follow orders in **B**, **C** and **D**.

B Check One	**MEDICAL INTERVENTIONS: Person has pulse <u>and/or</u> is breathing.** ☐ **COMFORT MEASURES ONLY** Use medication by any route, positioning, wound care and other measures to relieve pain and suffering. Use oxygen, oral suction and manual treatment of airway obstruction as needed for comfort. *Do not transfer to hospital for life-sustaining treatment. Transfer if comfort needs cannot be met in current location.* ☐ **LIMITED ADDITIONAL INTERVENTIONS** Includes care described above. Use medical treatment, IV fluids and cardiac monitor as indicated. Do not use intubation, advanced airway interventions, or mechanical ventilation. *Transfer to hospital if indicated. Avoid intensive care if possible.* ☐ **FULL TREATMENT** Includes care described above. Use intubation, advanced airway interventions, mechanical ventilation, and cardioversion as indicated. *Transfer to hospital if indicated. Includes intensive care.* *Additional Orders* _____

C Check One	**ANTIBIOTICS:** ☐ No antibiotics. Use other measures to relieve symptoms. ☐ Determine use or limitation of antibiotics when infection occurs, with comfort as goal ☐ Use antibiotics if life can be prolonged *Additional Orders*	**D** Check One	**ARTIFICIALLY ADMINISTERED HYDRATION / NUTRITION:** Always offer food and liquids by mouth if feasible ☐ No hydration and artificial nutrition by tube. ☐ Trial period of artificial hydration and nutrition by tube. ☐ Long-term artificial hydration and nutrition by tube. *Additional Orders*

E Check One	**SUMMARY OF GOALS, MEDICAL CONDITION AND SIGNATURES:** Discussed with ☐ Patient ☐ Parent of Minor ☐ Health Care Agent ☐ Health Care Representative ☐ Court-Appointed Guardian ☐ Other: Patient Goals/Medical Condition:

By signing this form, I acknowledge that this request regarding resuscitative measures is consistent with the known desires of, and in the best interest of, the individual who is the subject of the form.

Physician /PA/CRNP Printed Name:	Physician /PA/CRNP Phone Number
Physician/PA/CRNP Signature (Required):	DATE

Signature of Patient or Surrogate

Signature (required)	Name (print)	Relationship (write "self" if patient)

Other Contact Information

Surrogate	Relationship	Phone Number	
Health Care Professional Preparing Form	Preparer Title	Phone Number	Date Prepared

Directions for Healthcare Professionals

Any individual for whom a Pennsylvania Order for Life-Sustaining Treatment form is completed should ideally have an advance health care directive that provides instructions for the individual's health care and appoints an agent to make medical decisions whenever the patient is unable to make or communicate a healthcare decision. If the patient wants a DNR Order issued in section "A", the physician/PA/CRNP should discuss the issuance of an Out-of-Hospital DNR order, if the individual is eligible, to assure that an EMS provider can honor his/her wishes. Contact the Pennsylvania Department of Aging for information about sample forms for advance health care directives. Contact the Pennsylvania Department of Health, Bureau of EMS, for information about Out-of Hospital Do-Not-Resuscitate orders, bracelets and necklaces. POLST forms may be obtained online from the Pennsylvania Department of Health.   www.health.state.pa.us

Completing POLST

Must be completed by a health care professional based on patient preferences and medical indications or decisions by the patient or a surrogate. This document refers to the person for whom the orders are issued as the "individual" or "patient" and refers to any other person authorized to make healthcare decisions for the patient covered by this document as the "surrogate."

At the time a POLST is completed, any current advance directive, if available, must be reviewed.

Must be signed by a physician/PA/CRNP and patient/surrogate to be valid. Verbal orders are acceptable with follow-up signature by physician/PA/CRNP in accordance with facility/community policy. A person designated by the patient or surrogate may document the patient's or surrogate's agreement. Use of original form is strongly encouraged. Photocopies and Faxes of signed POLST forms should be respected where necessary

Using POLST

If a person's condition changes and time permits, the patient or surrogate must be contacted to assure that the POLST is updated as appropriate.

If any section is not completed, then the healthcare provider should follow other appropriate methods to determine treatment.

An automated external defibrillator (AED) should not be used on a person who has chosen "Do Not Attempt Resuscitation"

Oral fluids and nutrition must always be offered if medically feasible.

When comfort cannot be achieved in the current setting, the person, including someone with "comfort measures only," should be transferred to a setting able to provide comfort (e.g., treatment of a hip fracture).

A person who chooses either "comfort measures only" or "limited additional interventions" may not require transfer or referral to a facility with a higher level of care.

An IV medication to enhance comfort may be appropriate for a person who has chosen "Comfort Measures Only."

Treatment of dehydration is a measure which may prolong life. A person who desires IV fluids should indicate "Limited Additional Interventions" or "Full Treatment.

A patient with or without capacity or the surrogate who gave consent to this order or who is otherwise specifically authorized to do so, can revoke consent to any part of this order providing for the withholding or withdrawal of life-sustaining treatment, at any time, and request alternative treatment.

Review

This form should be reviewed periodically (consider at least annually) and a new form completed if necessary when:
(1) The person is transferred from one care setting or care level to another, or
(2) There is a substantial change in the person's health status, or
(3) The person's treatment preferences change.

Revoking POLST

If the POLST becomes invalid or is replaced by an updated version, draw a line through sections A through E of the invalid POLST, write "VOID" in large letters across the form, and sign and date the form.

CHAPTER 11
FORM 8: DURABLE POWER OF ATTORNEY

FORM 8 LETS PERSON GIVE POWER TO SOMEONE TO ACT FOR THEM

This form lets a person give power to someone. Half the form is warning language set by law.

FORM CAN SHARE POWER WITH "AGENT" TO LET THEM ACT FOR THEM

This form lets a person (called "Principal") give power to someone to act for them (called "Agent" or "Attorney-in-Fact"). Often a spouse or friend is named to let them go and pay bills, use accounts, sell property, and see records for a person who is sick, away, or busy. This may avoid a guardianship or nursing home. A person still has power to do things and to overrule an Agent. Those using a form should say so and show it, like writing "Joy Wu, Agent acting under a Power of Attorney for Ed Wu".

FORM IS DURABLE AND GIVES MOST POWERS BUT NOT UNUSUAL POWERS

This book's form is called "Durable" since it can be used even if a person is incapacitated, but power given ends on a person's death. This book's form is valid when signed and is not "springing" effective only on an event. Some forms have "successor agents" or "coagents" but this can have legal problems. This book's form gives broad power and also lists some specific powers (words in state law helpfully further explain these) but unusual powers that need special words to give are not given (like special power to make big gifts, to decline to accept property, and power to do a Will is not given).

FORM IS DANGEROUS AND UNUSUAL ACTS MAY BE IMPROPER

This form is rarely used because it lets the named Agent do dangerous things like sell a person's property, take from accounts, borrow money, and agree to binding contracts. An Agent has a legal duty to act in "best interests" of a person and follow instructions and keep records, but misconduct may not be seen until too late. The law is complex but it may be against the law for an Agent to gift away things or do unusual actions, and <u>if gifting or unusual actions might be done a lawyer may be needed</u>.

DO FORM WITH 2 WITNESSES AND A NOTARY, AND LATER DO OTHER PAGES

The form is done by a person signing the main part with 2 witnesses and a notary. Witnesses should be over 18 and not named Agent in a form. There is also a "Notice" warnings page for the person doing the form to sign, and an "Acknowledgment Executed By Agent" warnings page for the Agent to sign anytime later. Usually the Agent is given the completed form or it can be kept by a person or their spouse and only handed out if needed. A form can be revoked by a verbal or written notice to an Agent, and others who might still follow the form should be told about revocation.

FORM 8:
DURABLE POWER OF ATTORNEY

<u>NOTICE</u>

(FOR DURABLE POWER OF ATTORNEY)

THE PURPOSE OF THIS POWER OF ATTORNEY IS TO GIVE THE PERSON YOU DESIGNATE (YOUR "AGENT") BROAD POWERS TO HANDLE YOUR PROPERTY, WHICH MAY INCLUDE POWERS TO SELL OR OTHERWISE DISPOSE OF ANY REAL OR PERSONAL PROPERTY WITHOUT ADVANCE NOTICE TO YOU OR APPROVAL BY YOU.

THIS POWER OF ATTORNEY DOES NOT IMPOSE A DUTY ON YOUR AGENT TO EXERCISE GRANTED POWERS, BUT, WHEN POWERS ARE EXERCISED, YOUR AGENT MUST USE DUE CARE TO ACT FOR YOUR BENEFIT AND IN ACCORDANCE WITH THIS POWER OF ATTORNEY.

YOUR AGENT MAY EXERCISE THE POWERS GIVEN HERE THROUGHOUT YOUR LIFETIME, EVEN AFTER YOU BECOME INCAPACITATED, UNLESS YOU EXPRESSLY LIMIT THE DURATION OF THESE POWERS OR YOU REVOKE THESE POWERS OR A COURT ACTING ON YOUR BEHALF TERMINATES YOUR AGENT'S AUTHORITY.

YOUR AGENT MUST ACT IN ACCORDANCE WITH YOUR REASONABLE EXPECTATIONS TO THE EXTENT ACTUALLY KNOWN BY YOUR AGENT AND, OTHERWISE, IN YOUR BEST INTEREST, ACT IN GOOD FAITH AND ACT ONLY WITHIN THE SCOPE OF AUTHORITY GRANTED BY YOU IN THE POWER OF ATTORNEY.

THE LAW PERMITS YOU, IF YOU CHOOSE, TO GRANT BROAD AUTHORITY TO AN AGENT UNDER POWER OF ATTORNEY, INCLUDING THE ABILITY TO GIVE AWAY ALL OF YOUR PROPERTY WHILE YOU ARE ALIVE OR TO SUBSTANTIALLY CHANGE HOW YOUR PROPERTY IS DISTRIBUTED AT YOUR DEATH. BEFORE SIGNING THIS DOCUMENT, YOU SHOULD SEEK THE ADVICE OF AN ATTORNEY AT LAW TO MAKE SURE YOU UNDERSTAND IT.

A COURT CAN TAKE AWAY THE POWERS OF YOUR AGENT IF IT FINDS YOUR AGENT IS NOT ACTING PROPERLY.

THE POWERS AND DUTIES OF AN AGENT UNDER A POWER OF ATTORNEY ARE EXPLAINED MORE FULLY IN 20 PA.C.S. CH. 56.

IF THERE IS ANYTHING ABOUT THIS FORM THAT YOU DO NOT UNDERSTAND, YOU SHOULD ASK A LAWYER OF YOUR OWN CHOOSING TO EXPLAIN IT TO YOU.

I HAVE READ OR HAD EXPLAINED TO ME THIS NOTICE AND I UNDERSTAND ITS CONTENTS.

_____   _____

PRINCIPAL   **DATE**

DURABLE POWER OF ATTORNEY

I _____ (insert name and address) make this power of attorney document as the principal and do hereby appoint as my agent _____ (insert the name and address of the person appointed), and I hereby give this agent all the power and authority I possess or may give and they may do any act, deed, matter, or thing as I could do if I were personally present except as limited by Pennsylvania or other law.

This power of attorney will continue to be effective even though I become incapacitated, disabled, or incompetent. This document is not affected by uncertainty if I am alive.

This instrument is effective immediately.

I agree any third party who receives a copy of this document may act under it. I agree to indemnify any third party for any claims that arise because of reliance on this power of attorney. Revocation is not effective as to a third party until they learn of the revocation.

Without limited any grant of power or authority, I specifically give my agent in this document the following power and authority:

To engage in tangible personal property transactions.

To engage in banking and financial transactions.

To engage in stock, bond and other securities transactions.

To engage in commodity and option transactions.

To engage in real property transactions.

To borrow money.

To enter safe deposit boxes.

To engage in insurance and annuity transactions.

To engage in retirement plan transactions.

To handle interests in estates and trusts.

To pursue claims and litigation.

To receive government benefits.

To pursue tax matters.

To make limited gifts.

To create a trust for my benefit.

To make additions to an existing trust for my benefit.

To claim an elective share of the estate of my deceased spouse.

To authorize my admission to a medical, nursing, residential or similar facility and to enter into agreements for my care.

To renounce fiduciary positions.

To withdraw and receive the income or corpus of a trust.

(Optional) I hereby limit or extend the power and authority given my agent in this document, which shall control over any other provision, as follows: _____

_____

_____

_____.

PRINCIPAL

I willfully and voluntarily sign this document as principal and I understand its purpose.

Signed this ___ day of _____, 20___.

_____
Principal's Signature

WITNESSES

This document was signed in our presence and the person who signed this document as principal appears to be of sound mind and to be making this designation voluntarily, without duress, fraud, or undue influence, and we sign below as witnesses.

Witness Signature: _____   Witness Signature: _____
Print Name: _____   Print Name: _____

NOTARY

On this ___ day of _____, 20__, before me personally appeared the above-named principal who is satisfactorily proven to be the person named principal, who then executed this document as principal and acknowledged doing so.

In witness whereof, I hereunto set my hand and official seals.

_____
Notary

ACKNOWLEDGMENT EXECUTED BY AGENT

I,_____, HAVE READ THE ATTACHED POWER OF
ATTORNEY AND AM THE PERSON IDENTIFIED AS THE AGENT FOR THE
PRINCIPAL. I HEREBY ACKNOWLEDGE THAT WHEN I ACT AS AGENT:

I SHALL ACT IN ACCORDANCE WITH THE PRINCIPAL'S REASONABLE
EXPECTATIONS TO THE EXTENT ACTUALLY KNOWN BY ME AND,
OTHERWISE, IN THE PRINCIPAL'S BEST INTEREST, ACT IN GOOD FAITH AND
ACT ONLY WITHIN THE SCOPE OF AUTHORITY GRANTED TO ME BY THE
PRINCIPAL IN THE POWER OF ATTORNEY.

_____   _____

AGENT   DATE

CHAPTER 12
FORM 9: MEDICAL CONSENT AUTHORIZATION (FOR CHILD)

FORM GIVES POWER OVER CHILD'S MEDICAL CARE TO SOMEONE

Form 9 is a standard form by the state legislature found in law at 11 Pa.C.S. § 2513 that lets parents give power to someone to control a child's health care. The standard form lets a legal guardian or custodian also give power, has room for only 1 child, and has no space for the person given power to sign but this book's form changes these things to make the form easier to use.

FORM MAY REDUCE MEDICAL RISKS TO CHILD OR JUST HELP WITH CARE

This form lets a relative or family friend a parent names control and consent a child's health care. This form can greatly help since after emergency health care is given further care of a child under 18 is stopped while parents are contacted, and this delay may turn out to cause more risk or pain. Also giving power to someone may take pressure off parents by letting other persons make big decisions or make small decisions that ongoing care often creates. This form is often done "just in case" or "for safety" because a child will be away from parents and with a babysitter, nanny, teacher, relative, or medical person, for a reason like travel, vacation, school, medical treatment, parent's incarceration, or work. There is no minimum time period but a form is not usually done for babysitting or short trips when chance of needing the form is small. Some people to be more safe especially if another state may be involved do a Durable Power of Attorney (like Form 8) and there give a child's name and date of birth and give power to control and consent to medical, dental, and surgical examination and treatment.

WITH FORM PARENTS STILL HAVE POWER AND CONTROL AND CAN REVOKE

Even if the form is done parents retain power to make health care decisions and can override any other person, and a parent can revoke the form by giving written or verbal notice to the person named in a form, and usually telling others who saw and might still follow the form.

FORM IS SIGNED BEFORE 2 WITNESSES

The Medical Consent Authorization form is signed by the person giving power (1 parent signing is enough but 2 parents signing is better) before 2 witnesses who also sign. The witnesses should be at least 18 and not named in the form. The person given power must sign the form before they act.

FORM 9:
MEDICAL CONSENT AUTHORIZATION (FOR CHILD)

MEDICAL CONSENT AUTHORIZATION
(FOR CHILD UNDER THE MEDICAL CONSENT ACT)

I _____ (name) am the parent of the child(ren) listed below and there are no court orders now in effect that would prohibit me from conferring the power to consent upon another person.

I, _____, do hereby confer upon _____, residing at _____ the power to consent to necessary medical or mental health treatment for the following child(ren):

_____, residing at

_____, born on _____,

_____, residing at

_____, born on _____,

_____, residing at

_____, born on _____,

and on the child(ren)'s behalf do hereby state that the power to consent which I confer shall not be affected by my subsequent disability or incapacity.

The power which I confer is specifically limited to health care and mental health care decision making, and it may be exercised only by the person named above.

The person named above may consent to the child(ren)'s (cross out all that do not apply): medical, dental, surgical, developmental and/or mental health examination or treatment and may have access to any and all records, including, but not limited to, insurance records regarding any such services.

I confer the power to consent freely and knowingly in order to provide for the child(ren) and not as a result of pressure, threats or payments by any person or agency. This document shall remain in effect until it is revoked by notifying my child(ren)'s medical, mental health care and insurance providers, in writing, and the person named above that I wish to revoke it.

IN WITNESS WHEREOF, I, _____, have signed my named to this medical consent authorization, on this ___ day of _____, 20___, in _____, Pennsylvania.

_____   _____
(Printed Name)   (Signature)

_____
(Witness Signature)   (Witness No. 1 printed Name and Address)

_____
(Witness Signature)   (Witness No. 2 printed Name and Address)

ACCEPTANCE. I accept the power given in this form. Signed: _____

CHAPTER 13
FORM 10: STATEMENT OF CONTRARY INTENT
(FOR BODY)

FORM LETS PERSON NAME AGENT AND GIVE ORDERS FOR AFTER DEATH

Form 10 is written to comply with state law 20 Pa. C.S. § 305 to let a person name someone to control their dead body and related matters and if wanted give instructions for these things.

INSTEAD OF FAMILY CAN STATE "CONTRARY INTENT" TO NAME ANOTHER

If this form is not done by law a spouse or if no spouse closest family like a child control a person's dead body and related matters like funeral, but in a form a "contrary intent" other than this can be said. Some people choose a friend to not burden family at a time they will be upset, or they have wishes family may not follow. The person named in the form controls the dead body and all related matters.

IN FORM CAN GIVE INSTRUCTIONS

In the form a person can if wanted give instructions for any named agent or for family to follow. But many people skip most instructions and just trust the person in charge to follow things said to them or to act wisely. Some people to reduce overspending by family say things like, "I want the simplest funeral and burial reasonably possible". Some people during life make arrangements with funeral homes, cemeteries, and other places, which usually must legally be followed since this shows what a person wanted. It is recommended people discuss their wishes with family and friends.

NO MATTER WHAT A DECEDENT'S ESTATE PROPERTY AND MONEY PAYS

No matter who is in charge a decedent's estate's property and money pays for handling the body, funeral, and related things. It can greatly help if the person who is executor is the person named in this form. If there is not enough in the estate to pay things may not be done. A person should consider other people are free to decline to do things, like decline to speak or let their place or item be used.

COMPLETE FORM BY SIGNING AND DATING

To be valid the form must be dated and signed, and there is room for 2 witnesses to sign which is optional and makes the form more likely to be followed. The form can be given to the person named in the form or kept in a place it will be found quickly after death (or tell people where it is). To revoke a form a person just tells this to the person named in the form, and usually throw away or mark the form.

FORM 10:
STATEMENT OF CONTRARY INTENT (FOR BODY)

STATEMENT OF CONTRARY INTENT
(FOR BODY)

I, _____, appoint _____, as my agent for disposition of my body and related matters, and I give my agent and all other persons the instructions written below as authorized by 20 Pa. C. S. § 305 or other laws.

My agent shall have the sole right to determine disposition of my body after my death, including by burial, cremation, or any other form of disposition. No other person regardless of their kinship status to me or status as my spouse shall override my agent.

If I do not give instructions below to the person I appointed they still shall have the power, authority, rights, and privileges I described above and as provided them by law.

My agent shall follow instructions to the degree they can be reasonably accomplished and I have provided sufficient funds and property to pay for things (I understand I may leave areas blank):

    I want to have my body handled in the following manner concerning place, coffin, shroud , cremation, embalming, container, tombstone, or similar issues:

_____
_____
_____
_____
_____.

    I direct the following ceremony, service, wake, visitation, readings, events, or similar:

_____
_____
_____
_____.

    I have the following other instructions, requests, reminders, thanks, or similar:

_____
_____
_____.

(attach additional sheets as necessary)

_____   _____
Signature   Date
Signature of Witnesses (optional)

_____   _____

APPENDIX A:
HOW TO DOWNLOAD LEGAL FORMS

TO GET FORMS PEOPLE CAN (1) DOWNLOAD FORMS FREE AS EXPLAINED ON THIS PAGE, OR (2) PHOTOCOPY BOOK PAGES. BOOK BUYERS ARE AUTHORIZED TO DOWNLOAD AND COPY FORMS FOR THEIR OWN AND THEIR FAMILY'S USE.

FILES TO DOWNLOAD ARE IN BOTH:

1) PDF FORMAT WHERE NO CHANGES CAN BE MADE BUT IT CAN BE PRINTED, AND

2) WORD FORMAT WHERE CHANGES CAN BE MADE BY TYPING IN WORDS AND IT CAN BE PRINTED.

DOWNLOAD FORMS AT THESE LINKS:

ge.tt/6R4f6uD2

ge.tt/5psr8uD2/v/0 (DOC file)

ge.tt/2rzbBuD2/v/0   (PDF file)

app.box.com/s/c2l4exlbuz5k4p4ei7wgz4dg523r7lkq

app.box.com/s/qi1j77upr3ebdy0aeulhcls9lpnwlmke (DOC file)

mediafire.com/?5aqhqc7b5x4eh3b   (DOC file)

mediafire.com/?4blkkts2jmme72n (PDF file)

4shared.com/folder/y78mabH1/penn.html

EMAIL ANY COMMENTS TO DAVENPORTPRESS@GMAIL.COM .

APPENDIX B:
SAMPLE FILLED OUT LEGAL FORMS

The rest of this book has sample filled out legal forms including sample Wills.

All forms in this book can be filled out by pen or marker (and most people do this), and using a computer or typewriter to neatly complete forms is not legally required.

All signatures and dates by signatures should be handwritten with permanent pen or marker and not done by a computer or typewriter.

People need not worry about neatness or small mistakes since a document is usually fine if those people who knew a decedent in life can tell the likely meaning.

For forms with blank lines people can type or handwrite words into these however wanted, and can:

   1) type in (or handwrite) words into a line ("I appoint ___John Doe____ as Agent"),

   2) use underlining so added words look underlined, maybe using whited out commas to hold underlining ("I appoint __John Doe__ as Agent"), or

   3) remove blank lines so it looks like normal text ("I appoint John Doe as Agent"), but removing lines can make added words hard to see so some people put added words in bold ("I appoint **John Doe** as Agent").

SAMPLE FILLED OUT LEGAL FORMS

SAMPLE FILLED OUT
FORM 1:
LAST WILL AND TESTAMENT (WITH GUARDIANS)

LAST WILL AND TESTAMENT

I, ____Henry James Ford____, a resident of __Lehigh__ County, Pennsylvania, hereby make, publish, and declare this as my Last Will and Testament (called here my "Will"), and I hereby revoke any Wills and Codicils earlier made by me.

1. GIFTS. I give the following gifts which are specific gifts except any gifts of money amounts are general gifts:

I give ____1.5 carat diamond____ to _Ruth Ann Jones_ if they survive me;

I give _63 Ivy Road, Lundy, Pennsylvania, including land, buildings, and fixtures_ to ____Greta Olivia Parupski____ they survive me;

I give ____$7,281.35____ to _Wanda Kay Zinski_ if they survive me;

I give __Irish engraved ring__ to _Harriet Rush Smith_ if they survive me;

I give _all jewelry not given above_ to _Hannah Eve Pidoski_ if they survive me;

I give _UBank account ending #8923_ to _John Kent my cousin_ if they survive me;

I give _antique oak tables and chairs, grandfather clock, and all lamps_ to _Anne Janet Lynn-Hutchinson_ if they survive me;

I give _1998 Ford truck_ to _John Hatcher my cousin_ if they survive me; and

I give _____ to _____ if they survive me.

2. TANGIBLE PERSONAL PROPERTY WRITINGS. I may leave signed writings giving tangible personal property written before or after this Will. I direct such writings and gifts in them be incorporated by reference into this Will or treated as legally binding by other means including because they are made with testamentary intent. But if property is specifically given in this Will a contrary gift in such writings has no effect. Any such writings are not revoked by this Will. Any such writings and gifts in them not found by 60 days after my death shall have no effect. A recipient getting property in such writings must survive me by 60 days for a gift to them to have any effect. Several such writings are intended as and should be construed as a single document to all be followed. If the same property is given in multiple writings the more recently done page shall control.

3. RESIDUE. I give all my property and estate remaining and not given or used by other Will provisions or other ways, whether now owned or later acquired, wherever located, and of any kind and nature including personal, real, and mixed property, including the rest, residue, and remainder of my estate (all of which is called in this Will the "residue"), as follows: to_Mary Jennifer Ford my wife_____ if they survive me, but if they all do not survive me I give the just described property to _Eric James Ford and Wendy Sue Hanson my children_____ or their lineal descendants per stirpes. Part of this residue section may be left unfilled, and any used part should be given effect.

4. ADMINISTRATION. I name and appoint ___Mary Jennifer Ford my wife___ as executor of my Will and my estate.

5. GUARDIANS. If any of my children have not reached age 18 I name and appoint ___Margaret Kim Windsor my sister_____ to be guardian of the person of such children. I also name and appoint ___Margaret Kim Windsor___ as guardian of the estate for such children and their estate and property, and also for any other persons under age 18 who receive or possess property and their estate and property.

6. MISCELLANEOUS. The following applies to this Will and generally.

I request unsupervised and informal administration and probate of my estate and Will.

Plural, singular, or gender meanings do not limit any Will part, such as use of "they".

Any executor or guardian of any type acting under this Will or otherwise shall serve without bond, surety, or other security including for performance of their duties.

An executor shall sell a gift unless all beneficiaries getting it agree on its use or sale.

No unfilled Will part is a mistake, and Will parts about the residue may be left blank.

The priority of Will gifts of the same type is based on the order they appear.

The words "give" and "gift" mean the same as devise, bequest, grant, legacy or similar.

The words "survive" or "surviving" in a gift or other place creates an absolute condition that must be met or a gift fails and anti-lapse laws or similar have no effect.

Any person or entity not surviving me by 60 days shall be deemed to not survive me.

For gifts to multiple beneficiaries a non-surviving beneficiary's share goes to other beneficiaries in proportion to shares they are taking, including for the residue or if a gift requires or mentions survival, but not if an alternate beneficiary is provided in the Will.

Any executor and guardian of any type is given as much power, authority, and discretion that may be given by law, including power to (with no liability for change in value) sell, lease, assign, mortgage, invest, operate, hold, exchange, and transfer in any way any property including of the estate, settle claims for and against the estate or any person, do any tax action or filing, and have power of sale for real property, all with no need for act of any court or party, and all with no need for any filing or inventory.

Any executor has power to take any action involving an ancillary estate, give different kinds, portions or undivided interests in property to beneficiaries and assign value to all things, and do any distribution or division of my estate or property in cash or in kind.

Any executor may any time and in any amount pay debts of mine or my estate they in their sole and absolute discretion finds are valid, enforceable, timely, and fair, including of a last illness, for funeral and related things, with no filing or act of court or other party.

For property or other thing going to minors an executor without act of court has power to transfer property to: the minor, any adult the minor lives with, a guardian of the estate named by Will or a court, or a custodian under the Pennsylvania Uniform Transfers to Minors Act or similar law. For such minors the person named guardian of the estate in this Will is nominated and named as custodian under the Pennsylvania Uniform Transfers to Minors Act or similar law, or if needed any executor may name a custodian.

Any successor including of an executor or guardian of any type named in this Will shall have all powers, privileges, immunities and exemptions their predecessor had.

My not giving more to children and other family is intentional and not a mistake.

Residue includes lapsed or failed gifts, insurance paid to the estate, inheritances owed testator, and property testator had power of appointment or testamentary disposition over.

TESTATOR

I have signed this my Last Will and Testament this __19th__ day of ___January__ , 20 __16__ .

Henry James Ford
Testator

WITNESSES

Signed by ____Henry James Ford_____ , the Testator, as the Last Will and Testament of the Testator, in the presence of both of us, who, at Testator's request and in Testator's presence and the presence of each other, have signed our names as witnesses.

Amy Janet Windsor	____87 Main Street, Pottsville, PA 19402____
Witness	Address
Brian Adam Smith	__6328 Forest Lane, Norristown, PA 19403__
Witness	Address

SAMPLE FILLED OUT
FORM 2:
LAST WILL AND TESTAMENT (NO GUARDIANS)

LAST WILL AND TESTAMENT

I, **Ruth Miranda Kent** a resident of **Schuylkill** County, Pennsylvania, hereby make, publish, and declare this as my Last Will and Testament (called here my "Will"), and I hereby revoke any Wills and Codicils earlier made by me.

1. GIFTS. I give the following gifts which are specific gifts except any gifts of money amounts are general gifts:

I give a total of $100,000 to: 50% to Abraham Daniel Walker, 40% to Amy Ann Hope, and 10% to Jennifer Kim Beaufort   if they survive me;

I give $900 and my cat Bob to Wanda Gina Sorenson if she survives me;

I give 1987 Ford Truck and any other vehicles I own of any type to Reginald William Porter my nephew if they survive me;

I give $20,000 to Greg Paul Best but if they fail to survive me then to his wife Mary Gertrude Best;

I give $990 to each of my first cousins if they survive me;

I give $5,000 to St. Mary Angelica of the Cross which was my old church in Allentown if they survive me;

I give $2,250 to St. Joseph's my church if they survive me;.

I give $300 to Timmy Hart my paperboy if they survive me;

I give $20,000 to Juanita Chuzappa my helper but if they fail to survive me then to Juanita's Chuzappa's children;

I give $10,000 to Marion Dexter my neighbor but if they fail to survive me then to her husband Arthur Dexter; and

I give $10,000 total to Janet Wilkins, Miranda Britom, Cindy Spagor, Diana Linda Craigtown, and Teresa Germann if they survive me.

2. TANGIBLE PERSONAL PROPERTY WRITINGS. I may leave signed writings giving tangible personal property written before or after this Will. I direct such writings and gifts in them be incorporated by reference into this Will or treated as legally binding by other means including because they are made with testamentary intent. But if property is specifically given in this Will a contrary gift in such writings has no effect. Any such writings are not revoked by this Will. Any such writings and gifts in them not found by 60 days after my death shall have no effect. A recipient getting property in such writings must survive me by 60 days for a gift to them to have any effect. Several such writings are intended as and should be construed as a single document to all be followed. If the same property is given in multiple writings the more recently done page shall control.

3. RESIDUE. I give all my property and estate remaining and not given or used by other Will provisions or other ways, whether now owned or later acquired, wherever located, and of any kind and nature including personal, real, and mixed property, including the rest, residue, and remainder of my estate (all of which is called in this Will the "residue"), as follows: to **Wanda Kim Dallas my daughter** if they survive me, but if they all do not survive me then I give the just described property to **Jane Carol Yancy and Paul Alan Kent my cousins** or their lineal descendants per stirpes. Part of this residue section may be left unfilled, and any used part should be given effect.

4. ADMINISTRATION. I name and appoint **Wanda Kim Dallas my daughter** as executor of my Will and my estate.

5. MISCELLANEOUS. The following applies to this Will and generally.
　I request unsupervised and informal administration and probate of my estate and Will.
　Plural, singular, or gender meanings do not limit any Will part, such as use of "they".
　Any executor or guardian of any type acting under this Will or otherwise shall serve without bond, surety, or other security including for performance of their duties.
　An executor shall sell a gift unless all beneficiaries getting it agree on its use or sale.
　No unfilled Will part is a mistake, and Will parts about the residue may be left blank.
　The priority of Will gifts of the same type is based on the order they appear.
　The words "give" and "gift" mean the same as devise, bequest, grant, legacy or similar.
　The words "survive" or "surviving" in a gift or other place creates an absolute condition that must be met or a gift fails and anti-lapse laws or similar have no effect.
　Any person or entity not surviving me by 60 days shall be deemed to not survive me.
　For gifts to multiple beneficiaries a non-surviving beneficiary's share goes to other beneficiaries in proportion to shares they are taking, including for the residue or if a gift requires or mentions survival, but not if an alternate beneficiary is provided in the Will.
　Any executor and guardian of any type is given as much power, authority, and

discretion that may be given by law, including power to (with no liability for change in value) sell, lease, assign, mortgage, invest, operate, hold, exchange, and transfer in any way any property including of the estate, settle claims for and against the estate or any person, do any tax action or filing, and have power of sale for real property, all with no need for act of any court or party, and all with no need for any filing or inventory.

Any executor has power to take any action involving an ancillary estate, give different kinds, portions or undivided interests in property to beneficiaries and assign value to all things, and do any distribution or division of my estate or property in cash or in kind.

Any executor may any time and in any amount pay debts of mine or my estate they in their sole and absolute discretion finds are valid, enforceable, timely, and fair, including of a last illness, for funeral and related things, with no filing or act of court or other party.

For property or other thing going to minors an executor without act of court has power to transfer property to: the minor, any adult the minor lives with, a guardian of the estate named by Will or a court, or a custodian under the Pennsylvania Uniform Transfers to Minors Act or similar law. For such minors the person named guardian of the estate in this Will is nominated and named as custodian under the Pennsylvania Uniform Transfers to Minors Act or similar law, or if needed any executor may name a custodian.

Any successor including of an executor or guardian of any type named in this Will shall have all powers, privileges, immunities and exemptions their predecessor had.

My not giving more to children and other family is intentional and not a mistake.

Residue includes lapsed or failed gifts, insurance paid to the estate, inheritances owed testator, and property testator had power of appointment or testamentary disposition over.

TESTATOR

I have signed this my Last Will and Testament this _21st_ day of _March_, 20 _15_.

Ruth Miranda Kent
Testator

WITNESSES

Signed by ___Ruth Miranda Kent___, the Testator, as the Last Will and Testament of the Testator, in the presence of both of us, who, at Testator's request and in Testator's presence and the presence of each other, have signed our names as witnesses.

Susan Harriet Rogers	87 Badger Road, Carlisle, PA 17103
Witness	Address
Lucy Ann Pamway	892 Franklin Street, Harrisburg, PA 17201
Witness	Address

SAMPLE FILLED OUT
ADDITIONAL SAMPLE #2 OF FORM 1:
LAST WILL AND TESTAMENT (WITH GUARDIANS)

LAST WILL AND TESTAMENT

I, <u>Paul Eric Windsor a/k/a Petey Windsor</u> a resident of <u>Lancaster</u> County, Pennsylvania, hereby make, publish, and declare this as my Last Will and Testament (called here my "Will"), and I hereby revoke any Wills and Codicils earlier made by me.

1. GIFTS. I give the following gifts which are specific gifts except any gifts of money amounts are general gifts:

I give <u>$10,000</u> to <u>the United States Cancer Society</u> if they survive me.

I give <u>$5,000 in total</u> to <u>my cousin David Krupp's children</u> if they survive me.

I give <u>$6,000 in total</u> to <u>my cousin Carol Bown's children</u> if they survive me.

I give <u>$500 each</u> to <u>each of my grandchildren</u> if they survive me.

I give _____
to _____ if they survive me.

I give _____
to _____ if they survive me.

2. TANGIBLE PERSONAL PROPERTY WRITINGS. I may leave signed writings giving tangible personal property written before or after this Will. I direct such writings and gifts in them be incorporated by reference into this Will or treated as legally binding by other means including because they are made with testamentary intent. But if property is specifically given in this Will a contrary gift in such writings has no effect. Any such writings are not revoked by this Will. Any such writings and gifts in them not found by 60 days after my death shall have no effect. A recipient getting property in such writings must survive me by 60 days for a gift to them to have any effect. Several such writings are intended as and should be construed as a single document to all be followed. If the same property is given in multiple writings the more recently done page shall control.

75

3. RESIDUE. I give all my property and estate remaining and not given or used by other Will provisions or other ways, whether now owned or later acquired, wherever located, and of any kind and nature including personal, real, and mixed property, including the rest, residue, and remainder of my estate (all of which is called in this Will the "residue"), as follows: to _____
if they survive me, but if they all do not survive me I give the just described property to
    my children John Terry Windsor, Pamela Kay Smith, Martha Fiona Peterson, Greta Samantha Windsor-Somonis, Vernon Chester Windsor, and Mary Kay Windsor,
    and my loved cousin Beverly Hannah Carlson,_____
    and my great friend William Frank Sommenheim_____
or their lineal descendants per stirpes. Part of this residue section may be left unfilled, and any used part should be given effect.

4. ADMINISTRATION. I name and appoint __my son John Terry Windsor__ as executor of my Will and my estate.

5. GUARDIANS. If any of my children have not reached age 18 I name and appoint __John Terry Windsor__ to be guardian of the person of such children.   I also name and appoint __John Terry Windsor__ as guardian of the estate for such children and their estate and property, and also for any other persons under age 18 who receive or possess property and their estate and property.

6. MISCELLANEOUS. The following applies to this Will and generally.
    I request unsupervised and informal administration and probate of my estate and Will.
    Plural, singular, or gender meanings do not limit any Will part, such as use of "they".
    Any executor or guardian of any type acting under this Will or otherwise shall serve without bond, surety, or other security including for performance of their duties.
    An executor shall sell a gift unless all beneficiaries getting it agree on its use or sale.
    No unfilled Will part is a mistake, and Will parts about the residue may be left blank.
    The priority of Will gifts of the same type is based on the order they appear.
    The words "give" and "gift" mean the same as devise, bequest, grant, legacy or similar.
    The words "survive" or "surviving" in a gift or other place creates an absolute condition that must be met or a gift fails and anti-lapse laws or similar have no effect.
    Any person or entity not surviving me by 60 days shall be deemed to not survive me.
    For gifts to multiple beneficiaries a non-surviving beneficiary's share goes to other beneficiaries in proportion to shares they are taking, including for the residue or if a gift requires or mentions survival, but not if an alternate beneficiary is provided in the Will.

Any executor and guardian of any type is given as much power, authority, and discretion that may be given by law, including power to (with no liability for change in value) sell, lease, assign, mortgage, invest, operate, hold, exchange, and transfer in any way any property including of the estate, settle claims for and against the estate or any person, do any tax action or filing, and have power of sale for real property, all with no need for act of any court or party, and all with no need for any filing or inventory.

Any executor has power to take any action involving an ancillary estate, give different kinds, portions or undivided interests in property to beneficiaries and assign value to all things, and do any distribution or division of my estate or property in cash or in kind.

Any executor may any time and in any amount pay debts of mine or my estate they in their sole and absolute discretion finds are valid, enforceable, timely, and fair, including of a last illness, for funeral and related things, with no filing or act of court or other party.

For property or other thing going to minors an executor without act of court has power to transfer property to: the minor, any adult the minor lives with, a guardian of the estate named by Will or a court, or a custodian under the Pennsylvania Uniform Transfers to Minors Act or similar law. For such minors the person named guardian of the estate in this Will is nominated and named as custodian under the Pennsylvania Uniform Transfers to Minors Act or similar law, or if needed any executor may name a custodian.

Any successor including of an executor or guardian of any type named in this Will shall have all powers, privileges, immunities and exemptions their predecessor had.

My not giving more to children and other family is intentional and not a mistake.

Residue includes lapsed or failed gifts, insurance paid to the estate, inheritances owed testator, and property testator had power of appointment or testamentary disposition over.

TESTATOR

I have signed this my Last Will and Testament this 2nd day of ___July___, 20 15 .

Paul Eric Windsor
Testator

WITNESSES

Signed by _Paul Eric Windsor_ the Testator, as the Last Will and Testament of Testator, in the presence of both of us, who, at Testator's request and in Testator's presence and the presence of each other, have signed our names as witnesses.

Olivia Joy Pawlenty	87 Hastings Avenue, Lundy, PA 19403
Witness	Address
Roy Felix Pawlenty	87 Hastings Avenue, Lundy, PA 19403
Witness	Address

SAMPLE FILLED OUT
ADDITIONAL SAMPLE #2 OF FORM 2:
LAST WILL AND TESTAMENT (NO GUARDIANS)

LAST WILL AND TESTAMENT

I,___David Roger Widowonski___ , a resident of __Washington__ County, Pennsylvania, hereby make, publish, and declare this as my Last Will and Testament (called here my "Will"), and I hereby revoke any Wills and Codicils earlier made by me.

1. GIFTS. I give the following gifts which are specific gifts except any gifts of money amounts are general gifts.

I give __a total of $50,000__ to __Brian Oscar Peterson, Michael Paul Peterson, and Mary Rebecca Hart__ if they survive me.

I give __a total of $6,000__ to __Beth Tina Smith and Frank M. Smith__ if they survive me.

I give __$5,000__ to __Loretta Marsha Switt in the hope she will help her daughter Megan Kara Smith__ if they survive me.

I give __$3,000__ to __Loretta Marsha Switt__ if they survive me.

I give __Wells Fargo savings account ending in #8923__ to __Lawrence Deer__ if they survive me.

I give __$1,000__ to __American Red Cross charity__ if they survive me.

I give __$5,000__ to __Fishy Smith my fishing buddy__ if they survive me.

I give __$2,000__ to __Mary Nixon__ but is she does not survive me then to __Karen Kay Paulson__ .

I give __all cars and trucks I own at my death__ to __Victor Perez my mechanic__ if they survive me.

I give __$7,002.21__ to __Brenda Mary Hill but if she fails to survive me then to her brother William Matthew Hill__ .

2. TANGIBLE PERSONAL PROPERTY WRITINGS. I may leave signed writings giving tangible personal property written before or after this Will. I direct such writings and gifts in them be incorporated by reference into this Will or treated as legally binding by other means including because they are made with testamentary intent. But if property is specifically given in this Will a contrary gift in such writings has no effect. Any such writings are not revoked by this Will. Any such writings and gifts in them not found by 60 days after my death shall have no effect. A recipient getting property in such writings must survive me by 60 days for a gift to them to have any effect. Several such writings are intended as and should be construed as a single document to all be followed. If the same property is given in multiple writings the more recently done page shall control.

3. RESIDUE. I give all my property and estate remaining and not given or used by other Will provisions or other ways, whether now owned or later acquired, wherever located, and of any kind and nature including personal, real, and mixed property, including the rest, residue, and remainder of my estate (all of which is called in this Will the "residue"), as follows: to _____
if they survive me, but if they all do not survive me I give the just described property to

     20% to Hector Samuel Widowonski,
     30% to Kenneth Paul Widowonski, and
     50% to Mary Janet Maxwell

or their lineal descendants per stirpes. Part of this residue section may be left unfilled, and any used part should be given effect.

4. ADMINISTRATION. I name and appoint ___Hector Samuel Widowonski___ as executor of my Will and my estate.

5. MISCELLANEOUS. The following applies to this Will and generally.

    I request unsupervised and informal administration and probate of my estate and Will.

    Plural, singular, or gender meanings do not limit any Will part, such as use of "they".

    Any executor or guardian of any type acting under this Will or otherwise shall serve without bond, surety, or other security including for performance of their duties.

    An executor shall sell a gift unless all beneficiaries getting it agree on its use or sale.

    No unfilled Will part is a mistake, and Will parts about the residue may be left blank.

The priority of Will gifts of the same type is based on the order they appear.

The words "give" and "gift" mean the same as devise, bequest, grant, legacy or similar.

The words "survive" or "surviving" in a gift or other place creates an absolute condition that must be met or a gift fails and anti-lapse laws or similar have no effect.

Any person or entity not surviving me by 60 days shall be deemed to not survive me.

For gifts to multiple beneficiaries a non-surviving beneficiary's share goes to other beneficiaries in proportion to shares they are taking, including for the residue or if a gift requires or mentions survival, but not if an alternate beneficiary is provided in the Will.

Any executor and guardian of any type is given as much power, authority, and discretion that may be given by law, including power to (with no liability for change in value) sell, lease, assign, mortgage, invest, operate, hold, exchange, and transfer in any way any property including of the estate, settle claims for and against the estate or any person, do any tax action or filing, and have power of sale for real property, all with no need for act of any court or party, and all with no need for any filing or inventory.

Any executor has power to take any action involving an ancillary estate, give different kinds, portions or undivided interests in property to beneficiaries and assign value to all things, and do any distribution or division of my estate or property in cash or in kind.

Any executor may any time and in any amount pay debts of mine or my estate they in their sole and absolute discretion finds are valid, enforceable, timely, and fair, including of a last illness, for funeral and related things, with no filing or act of court or other party.

For property or other thing going to minors an executor without act of court has power to transfer property to: the minor, any adult the minor lives with, a guardian of the estate named by Will or a court, or a custodian under the Pennsylvania Uniform Transfers to Minors Act or similar law. For such minors the person named guardian of the estate in this Will is nominated and named as custodian under the Pennsylvania Uniform Transfers to Minors Act or similar law, or if needed any executor may name a custodian.

Any successor including of an executor or guardian of any type named in this Will shall have all powers, privileges, immunities and exemptions their predecessor had.

My not giving more to children and other family is intentional and not a mistake.

Residue includes lapsed or failed gifts, insurance paid to the estate, inheritances owed testator, and property testator had power of appointment or testamentary disposition over.

TESTATOR

I have signed this my Last Will and Testament this <u>31st</u> day of <u>March</u>, 20 <u>15</u>.

<u>*David Roger Widowsonki*</u>
Testator

WITNESSES

Signed by <u>David Roger Widowonski</u> the Testator, as the Last Will and Testament of Testator, in the presence of both of us, who, at Testator's request and in Testator's presence and the presence of each other, have signed our names as witnesses.

<u>*Michael Frank Bjerk*</u>   <u>87 Main Street, Madison, PA 19421</u>
Witness   Address

<u>*Brian Douglas Thorpe*</u>   <u>927 Hubert Street, Erie, PA 19405</u>
Witness   Address

SAMPLE FILLED OUT
FORM 3:
SELF-PROVING AFFIDAVIT

SELF-PROVING AFFIDAVIT

Acknowledgment

Commonwealth of Pennsylvania

County of __Lancaster__

    I, __John Henry Tescatone__, the testator whose name is signed to the attached or foregoing instrument, having been duly qualified according to law, do hereby acknowledge that I signed and executed the instrument as my Last Will; and that I signed it willingly and as my free and voluntary act for the purposes therein expressed.

    Sworn to or affirmed and acknowledged before me by __John Henry Tescatone__, the testator, this 16th day of __January__, 2016_.

John Henry Tescatone
(Testator)

Natalie Regina Notario
(Signature of officer)

NOTARY No. 3923733

(Seal and official capacity of officer)

Affidavit

Commonwealth of Pennsylvania

County of __Lancaster__

    We, __Mary Jennifer Bolger__, and __Karen Gina Kellogg__, the witnesses whose names are signed to the attached or foregoing instrument, being duly qualified according to law, do depose and say that we were present and saw the testator sign and execute the instrument as his Last Will; that the testator signed willingly and executed it as his free and voluntary act for the purposes therein expressed; that each subscribing witness in the hearing and sight of the testator signed the will as a witness; and that to the best of our knowledge the testator was at that time 18 or more years of age, of sound mind and under no constraint or undue influence.

    Sworn to or affirmed and subscribed to before me by __Mary Jennifer Bolger__, and __Karen Gina Kellogg__, witnesses, this 16th day of __January__, 2016_.

__Mary Jennifer Bolger__
Witness

__Karen Gina Kellogg__
Witness

Natalie Regina Notario
(Signature of officer)

NOTARY No. 3923733

(Seal and official capacity of officer)

84

SAMPLE FILLED OUT
FORM 4:
TANGIBLE PERSONAL PROPERTY LIST

TANGIBLE PERSONAL PROPERTY LIST

I intend and declare this writing makes gifts of tangible personal property to occur at my death. I make gifts below to recipients named next to property items but only if a recipient survives me by 60 days and if they do not then a gift has no effect. This list and gifts in it if not found by 60 days after my death shall have no effect. If property is specifically given in a Will a gift of such property here has no effect.

PROPERTY ITEMS GIFTED	NAMES OF RECIPIENTS
1998 Ford Truck	Samantha Bell
1.3 carat diamond ring	Abigail Sue Reed
Italian silver jewelry	Samantha Bell
14 ft power boat and kayak with paddles	Luke Mark Wheeler
Parkhurst-style bench	Rebecca Stewart
glass table and its wood chairs	Rebecca Stewart
set of 18 silver candlesticks	Mary and Cindy Lott
my wedding dress and shoes	Mary Lott
chainsaw with serial no. 382937	Larry Kelly
chainsaw with serial no. 89930484421	Brian Kelly
antique lanterns and repair kits for them	Jason Brooks
Tucker my pet dog and all his supplies	Susan Ditcher
oak lamp usually kept on porch	Susan Ditcher
all sewing machines and fabrics	Mary Kay Poppler
rocking chair bought in Oregon	Robert Schmidt
all fishing poles and fishing equipment	Elwood Blues
coin collection in 8 glass cases	Millard Filmore

DATE: __May 2, 2016__   SIGNED: *John William Filmore*

**SAMPLE FILLED OUT
FORM 5:
CODICIL**

CODICIL

I, ___Jennifer Kay Polka_, a resident of _Philadelphia_ County, Pennsylvania, declare this to be a Codicil to my Will dated __March 2, 2015_.

FIRST: I hereby do revoke the part of my Will that reads as follows:

_____ I give $20,000 to Paul Jacob Farmer if they survive me_____

_____ I give my 1967 Corvette to Ned Baker_____.

SECOND: I hereby do add the following part to my Will:

_____ I give $20,000 to Eve Susan Farmer if they survive me_____
_____.

THIRD: In all other respects I hereby do confirm and republish the above-described Will.

TESTATOR

IN WITNESS WHEREOF, I have set my hand and seal to this my Codicil, this _2nd_ day of __March__, 20_15_.

Jennifer Kay Polka
Testator

WITNESSES

We, the undersigned, declare in our presence the foregoing document was willingly published, declared, and signed by the above-named Testator as his or her Codicil, that to the best of our knowledge the Testator is at least 18 years of age and of sound mind and under no constraint or undue influence, that each of us is at least 18 years old, and that in the presence and hearing of Testator and each other we sign our names as witnesses.

Susan Vera Chomsky   88 Hunter Street, Silver Bay, PA 18103__
Witness   Address
Norman Paul Chomsky   88 Hunter Street, Silver Bay, PA 18103__
Witness   Address

SAMPLE FILLED OUT
FORM 6:
DURABLE HEALTH CARE POWER OF ATTORNEY AND
HEALTH CARE TREATMENT INSTRUCTIONS (LIVING WILL)

DURABLE HEALTH CARE POWER OF ATTORNEY AND HEALTH CARE TREATMENT INSTRUCTIONS (LIVING WILL)

PART I
INTRODUCTORY REMARKS ON
HEALTH CARE DECISION MAKING

You have the right to decide the type of health care you want.

Should you become unable to understand, make or communicate decisions about medical care, your wishes for medical treatment are most likely to be followed if you express those wishes in advance by:

(1) naming a health care agent to decide treatment for you; and
(2) giving health care treatment instructions to your health care agent or health care provider.

An advance health care directive is a written set of instructions expressing your wishes for medical treatment. It may contain a health care power of attorney, where you name a person called a "health care agent" to decide treatment for you, and a living will, where you tell your health care agent and health care providers your choices regarding the initiation, continuation, withholding or withdrawal of life-sustaining treatment and other specific directions.

You may limit your health care agent's involvement in deciding your medical treatment so that your health care agent will speak for you only when you are unable to speak for yourself or you may give your health care agent the power to speak for you immediately. This combined form gives your health care agent the power to speak for you only when you are unable to speak for yourself. A living will cannot be followed unless your attending physician determines that you lack the ability to understand, make or communicate health care decisions for yourself, and you are either permanently unconscious or you have an end-stage medical condition, which is a condition that will result in death despite the introduction or continuation of medical treatment. You, and not your health care agent, remain responsible for the cost of your medical care.

If you do not write down your wishes about your health care in advance, and if later you become unable to understand, make or communicate these decisions, those wishes may not be honored because they may remain unknown to others.

A health care provider who refuses to honor your wishes about health care must tell you of its refusal and help to transfer you to a health care provider who will honor your wishes.

You should give a copy of your advance health care directive (a living will, health care power of attorney or a document containing both) to your health care agent, your physicians, family members and others whom you expect would likely attend to your needs if you become unable to understand, make or communicate decisions about medical care. If your health care wishes change, tell your physician and write a new advance health care directive to replace your old one. It is important in selecting a health care agent that you choose a person you trust who is likely to be available in a medical situation where you cannot make decisions for yourself. You should inform that person that you have appointed him or her as your health care agent and discuss your beliefs and values with him or her so that your health care agent will understand your health care objectives.

You may wish to consult with knowledgeable, trusted individuals such as family members, your physician or clergy when considering an expression of your values and health care wishes. You are free to create your own advance health care directive to convey your wishes regarding medical treatment. The following form is an example of an advance health care directive that combines a health care power of attorney with a living will.

NOTES ABOUT THE USE OF THIS FORM

If you decide to use this form or create your own advance health care directive, you should consult with your physician and your attorney to make sure that your wishes are clearly expressed and comply with the law.

If you decide to use this form but disagree with any of its statements, you may cross out those statements.

You may add comments to this form or use your own form to help your physician or health care agent decide your medical care.

This form is designed to give your health care agent broad powers to make health care decisions for you whenever you cannot make them for yourself. It is also designed to express a desire to limit or authorize care if you have an end-stage medical condition or are permanently unconscious. If you do not desire to give your health care agent broad powers, or you do not wish to limit your care if you have an end-stage medical condition or are permanently unconscious, you may wish to use a different form or create your own. YOU SHOULD ALSO USE A DIFFERENT FORM IF YOU WISH TO EXPRESS YOUR PREFERENCES IN MORE DETAIL THAN THIS FORM ALLOWS OR IF YOU WISH FOR YOUR HEALTH CARE AGENT TO BE ABLE TO SPEAK FOR YOU IMMEDIATELY. In these situations, it is particularly important that you consult with your attorney and physician to make sure that your wishes are clearly expressed.

This form allows you to tell your health care agent your goals if you have an end-stage medical condition or other extreme and irreversible medical condition, such as advanced Alzheimer's disease. Do you want medical care applied aggressively in these situations or would you consider such aggressive medical care burdensome and undesirable?

You may choose whether you want your health care agent to be bound by your instructions or whether you want you health care agent to be able to decide at the time what course of treatment the health care agent thinks most fully reflects your wishes and values.

If you are a woman and diagnosed as being pregnant at the time a health care decision would otherwise be made pursuant to this form, the laws of this Commonwealth prohibit implementation of that decision if it directs that life-sustaining treatment, including nutrition and hydration, be withheld or withdrawn from you, unless your attending physician and an obstetrician who have examined you certify in your medical record that the life-sustaining treatments:

   (1) will not maintain you in such a way as to permit the continuing development and live birth of the unborn child;

   (2) will be physically harmful to you; or

   (3) will cause pain to you that cannot be alleviated by medication.

A physician is not required to perform a pregnancy test on you unless the physician has reason to believe that you may be pregnant.

Pennsylvania law protects your health care agent and health care providers from any legal liability for following in good faith your wishes as expressed in the form or by your health care agent's direction. It does not otherwise change professional standards or excuse negligence in the way your wishes are carried out. If you have any questions about the law, consult an attorney for guidance.

This form and explanation is not intended to take the place of specific legal or medical advice for which you should rely upon your own attorney and physician.

PART II
DURABLE HEALTH CARE POWER OF ATTORNEY

I __Mary Jennifer Peterson__ of __Montgomery__ County, Pennsylvania, appoint the person named below to be my health care agent to make health and personal care decisions for me.

Effective immediately and continuously until my death or revocation by a writing signed by me or someone authorized to make health care treatment decisions for me, I authorize all health care providers or other covered entities to disclose to my health care agent, upon my agent's request, any information, oral or written, regarding my physical or mental health, including, but not limited to, medical and hospital records and what is otherwise private, privileged, protected or personal health information, such as health information as defined and described in the Health Insurance Portability and Accountability Act of 1996 (Public Law 104—191, 110 Stat. 1936), the regulations promulgated thereunder and any other State or local laws and rules. Information disclosed by a health care provider or other covered entity may be redisclosed and may no longer be subject to the privacy rules provided by 45 C.F.R. Pt. 164.

The remainder of this document will take effect when and only when I lack the ability to understand, make or communicate a choice regarding a health or personal care decision as verified by my attending physician. My health care agent may not delegate the authority to make decisions.

MY HEALTH CARE AGENT HAS ALL OF THE FOLLOWING POWERS SUBJECT TO THE HEALTH CARE TREATMENT INSTRUCTIONS THAT FOLLOW IN PART III (CROSS OUT ANY POWERS YOU DO NOT WANT TO GIVE YOUR HEALTH CARE AGENT):

1. To authorize, withhold or withdraw medical care and surgical procedures.

2. To authorize, withhold or withdraw nutrition (food) or hydration (water) medically supplied by tube through my nose, stomach, intestines, arteries or veins.

3. To authorize my admission to or discharge from a medical, nursing, residential or similar facility and to make agreements for my care and health insurance for my care, including hospice and/or palliative care.

4. To hire and fire medical, social service and other support personnel responsible for my care.

5. To take any legal action necessary to do what I have directed.

6. To request that a physician responsible for my care issue a do-not-resuscitate (DNR) order, including an out-of-hospital DNR order, and sign any required documents   and consents.

APPOINTMENT OF HEALTH CARE AGENT

I appoint the following health care agent:

Health Care Agent: __Roger Frank Peterson   son__   (Name and relationship)

Address: __727 Evergreen Terrace, Harrisburg, PA 19402__

Telephone Number: Home __717-555-2028__ Work __715-555-9027__

E-Mail: __mjpeterson023820@gmail.com__

IF YOU DO NOT NAME A HEALTH CARE AGENT, HEALTH CARE PROVIDERS WILL ASK YOUR FAMILY OR AN ADULT WHO KNOWS YOUR PREFERENCES AND VALUES FOR HELP IN DETERMINING YOUR WISHES FOR TREATMENT. NOTE THAT YOU MAY NOT APPOINT YOUR DOCTOR OR OTHER HEALTH CARE PROVIDER AS YOUR HEALTH CARE AGENT UNLESS RELATED TO YOU BY BLOOD, MARRIAGE OR ADOPTION.

If my health care agent is not readily available or if my health care agent is my spouse and an action for divorce is filed by either of us after the date of this document, I appoint the person or persons named below in the order named. (It is helpful, but not required, to name alternative health care agents.)

First Alternative Health Care Agent: __Laurie Lynn Blom   daughent__ (Name and relationship)

Address: _927 Country Lane, Harrisburg, PA 19402_____

_____

Telephone Number: Home _610-555-2028_ Work _610-555-9027_

E-Mail: _____gogosteelers87@hotmail.com_____

Second Alternative Health Care Agent: _____ (Name and relationship)
Address: _____

_____

Telephone Number: Home _____ Work _____
E-Mail: _____

GUIDANCE FOR HEALTH CARE AGENT (OPTIONAL)
GOALS

If I have an end-stage medical condition or other extreme irreversible medical condition, my goals in making medical decisions are as follows (insert your personal priorities such as comfort, care, preservation of mental function, etc.): _____

_____

_____I trust my Heath Care Agent but if possible I would like to stay near Harrisburg and would like to stay with Doctor Kyle or Doctor Jensen._____

_____

_____

_____

_____

_____

_____

SEVERE BRAIN DAMAGE OR BRAIN DISEASE

If I should suffer from severe and irreversible brain damage or brain disease with no realistic hope of significant recovery, I would consider such a condition intolerable and the application of aggressive medical care to be burdensome. I therefore request that my health care agent respond to any intervening (other and separate) life-threatening conditions in the same manner as directed for an end-stage medical condition or state of permanent unconsciousness as I have indicated below.

Initials___*M.J.P.*___ I agree

Initials _____ I disagree

PART III

HEALTH CARE TREATMENT INSTRUCTIONS IN THE EVENT OF END-STAGE MEDICAL CONDITION OR PERMANENT UNCONSCIOUSNESS (LIVING WILL)

The following health care treatment instructions exercise my right to make my own health care decisions. These instructions are intended to provide clear and convincing evidence of my wishes to be followed when I lack the capacity to understand, make or communicate my treatment decisions:

IF I HAVE AN END-STAGE MEDICAL CONDITION (WHICH WILL RESULT IN MY DEATH, DESPITE THE INTRODUCTION OR CONTINUATION OF MEDICAL TREATMENT) OR AM PERMANENTLY UNCONSCIOUS SUCH AS AN IRREVERSIBLE COMA OR AN IRREVERSIBLE VEGETATIVE STATE AND THERE IS NO REALISTIC HOPE OF SIGNIFICANT RECOVERY, ALL OF THE FOLLOWING APPLY (CROSS OUT ANY TREATMENT INSTRUCTIONS WITH WHICH YOU DO NOT AGREE):

1. I direct that I be given health care treatment to relieve pain or provide comfort even if such treatment might shorten my life, suppress my appetite or my breathing, or be habit forming.

2. I direct that all life-prolonging procedures be withheld or withdrawn.

3. I specifically do not want any of the following as life prolonging procedures: (If you wish to receive any of these treatments, write "I do want" after the treatment)

heart-lung resuscitation (CPR) _____

mechanical ventilator (breathing machine) _____

dialysis (kidney machine) _____

surgery _____

chemotherapy _____

radiation treatment _____

antibiotics _____

Please indicate whether you want nutrition (food) or hydration (water) medically supplied by a tube into your nose, stomach, intestine, arteries, or veins if you have an end-stage medical condition or are permanently unconscious and there is no realistic hope of significant recovery.

(Initial only one statement).

TUBE FEEDINGS

_____ I want tube feedings to be given

OR

NO TUBE FEEDINGS

___M.J.P.___ I do not want tube feedings to be given.

HEALTH CARE AGENT'S USE OF INSTRUCTIONS
(INITIAL ONE OPTION ONLY)

_____ My health care agent must follow these instructions.

OR

___M.J.P.___ These instructions are only guidance. My health care agent shall have final say and may override any of my instructions. (Indicate any exceptions)_____

_____

_____

_____

If I did not appoint a health care agent, these instructions shall be followed.

LEGAL PROTECTION

Pennsylvania law protects my health care agent and health care providers from any legal liability for their good faith actions in following my wishes as expressed in this form or in complying with my health care agent's direction. On behalf of myself, my executors and heirs, I further hold my health care agent and my health care providers harmless and indemnify them against any claim for their good faith actions in recognizing my health care agent's authority or in following my treatment instructions.

ORGAN DONATION

(INITIAL ONE OPTION ONLY)

_____ I consent to donate my organs and tissues at the time of my death for the purpose of transplant, medical study or education. (Insert any limitations you desire on donation of specific organs or tissues or uses for donation of organs and tissues.) _____

OR

___M.J.P.___ I do not consent to donate my organs or tissues at the time of my death.

SIGNATURE

Having carefully read this document,I have signed it this __11th__ day of ___July___ , 20__15__ ,
revoking all previous health care powers of attorney and health care treatment instructions.

___*Mary Jennifer Peterson*___
(SIGN FULL NAME HERE FOR HEALTH CARE POWER OF
ATTORNEY AND HEALTH CARE TREATMENT INSTRUCTIONS.)

WITNESS: ___*Gary Brian Larson*___

WITNESS: ___*Sally Mae Burlington*___

Two witnesses at least 18 years of age are required by Pennsylvania law and should witness your signature in each other's presence. A person who signs this document on behalf of and at the direction of a principal may not be a witness. (It is preferable if the witnesses are not your heirs, nor your creditors, nor employed by any of your health care providers.)

NOTARIZATION (OPTIONAL)

(Notarization of document is not required by Pennsylvania law, but if the document is both witnessed and notarized, it is more likely to be honored by the laws of some other states.)

On this ___ day of_____, 20___, before me personally appeared the aforesaid declarant and principal, to me known to be the person described in and who executed the foregoing instrument and acknowledged that he/she executed the same as his/her free act and deed.

IN WITNESS WHEREOF, I have hereunto set my hand and affixed my official seal in the County of _____, State of _____ the day and year first above written.

_____
Notary Public

_____
My commission expires

SAMPLE FILLED OUT
FORM 7:
P.O.L.S.T. (DO NOT RESUSCITATE)

pennsylvania DEPARTMENT OF HEALTH	**Pennsylvania Orders for Life-Sustaining Treatment (POLST)**	Last Name **Smith**
		First/Middle Initial **John E**
		Date of Birth **Nov. 25, 1952**

FIRST follow these orders, **THEN** contact physician, certified registered nurse practitioner or physician assistant. This is an Order Sheet based on the person's medical condition and wishes at the time the orders were issued. Everyone shall be treated with dignity and respect.

A
Check One

CARDIOPULMONARY RESUSCITATION (CPR): Person has no pulse <u>and</u> is not breathing.

☐ CPR/Attempt Resuscitation   ☒ DNR/Do Not Attempt Resuscitation (Allow Natural Death)
When not in cardiopulmonary arrest, follow orders in **B**, **C** and **D**.

B
Check One

MEDICAL INTERVENTIONS: Person has pulse <u>and/or</u> is breathing.

☒ **COMFORT MEASURES ONLY** Use medication by any route, positioning, wound care and other measures to relieve pain and suffering. Use oxygen, oral suction and manual treatment of airway obstruction as needed for comfort. *Do not transfer* to hospital for life-sustaining treatment. *Transfer if comfort needs cannot be met in current location.*

☐ **LIMITED ADDITIONAL INTERVENTIONS** Includes care described above. Use medical treatment, IV fluids and cardiac monitor as indicated. Do not use intubation, advanced airway interventions, or mechanical ventilation.

Transfer to hospital if indicated. Avoid intensive care if possible.

☐ **FULL TREATMENT** Includes care described above. Use intubation, advanced airway interventions, mechanical ventilation, and cardioversion as indicated.

Transfer to hospital if indicated. Includes intensive care.

Additional Orders _____

C
Check One

ANTIBIOTICS:

☐ No antibiotics. Use other measures to relieve symptoms.
☒ Determine use or limitation of antibiotics when infection occurs, with comfort as goal
☐ Use antibiotics if life can be prolonged
Additional Orders

D
Check One

ARTIFICIALLY ADMINISTERED HYDRATION / NUTRITION:
Always offer food and liquids by mouth if feasible

☒ No hydration and artificial nutrition by tube.
☐ Trial period of artificial hydration and nutrition by tube.
☐ Long-term artificial hydration and nutrition by tube.
Additional Orders

E
Check One

SUMMARY OF GOALS, MEDICAL CONDITION AND SIGNATURES:

Discussed with
☒ Patient
☐ Parent of Minor
☐ Health Care Agent
☐ Health Care Representative
☐ Court-Appointed Guardian
☐ Other:

Patient Goals/Medical Condition:

By signing this form, I acknowledge that this request regarding resuscitative measures is consistent with the known desires of, and in the best interest of, the individual who is the subject of the form.

Physician /PA/CRNP Printed Name: **Dr. Frank Paul Colt**	Physician /PA/CRNP Phone Number **717-555-8493**
Physician/PA/CRNP Signature (Required): *Frank Paul Colt*	DATE **June 2, 2015**

Signature of Patient or Surrogate

Signature (required) *John Eric Smith*	Name (print) **John Eric Smith**	Relationship (write "self" if patient) **self**

PaDOH version 10-14-10

Other Contact Information

Surrogate	Relationship	Phone Number	
Health Care Professional Preparing Form	Preparer Title	Phone Number	Date Prepared

Directions for Healthcare Professionals

Any individual for whom a Pennsylvania Order for Life-Sustaining Treatment form is completed should ideally have an advance health care directive that provides instructions for the individual's health care and appoints an agent to make medical decisions whenever the patient is unable to make or communicate a healthcare decision. If the patient wants a DNR Order issued in section "A", the physician/PA/CRNP should discuss the issuance of an Out-of-Hospital DNR order, if the individual is eligible, to assure that an EMS provider can honor his/her wishes. Contact the Pennsylvania Department of Aging for information about sample forms for advance health care directives. Contact the Pennsylvania Department of Health, Bureau of EMS, for information about Out-of-Hospital Do-Not-Resuscitate orders, bracelets and necklaces. POLST forms may be obtained online from the Pennsylvania Department of Health.   www.health.state.pa.us

Completing POLST

Must be completed by a health care professional based on patient preferences and medical indications or decisions by the patient or a surrogate. This document refers to the person for whom the orders are issued as the "individual" or "patient" and refers to any other person authorized to make healthcare decisions for the patient covered by this document as the "surrogate."

At the time a POLST is completed, any current advance directive, if available, must be reviewed.

Must be signed by a physician/PA/CRNP and patient/surrogate to be valid. Verbal orders are acceptable with follow-up signature by physician/PA/CRNP in accordance with facility/community policy. A person designated by the patient or surrogate may document the patient's or surrogate's agreement. Use of original form is strongly encouraged. Photocopies and Faxes of signed POLST forms should be respected where necessary

Using POLST

If a person's condition changes and time permits, the patient or surrogate must be contacted to assure that the POLST is updated as appropriate.

If any section is not completed, then the healthcare provider should follow other appropriate methods to determine treatment.

An automated external defibrillator (AED) should not be used on a person who has chosen "Do Not Attempt Resuscitation"

Oral fluids and nutrition must always be offered if medically feasible.

When comfort cannot be achieved in the current setting, the person, including someone with "comfort measures only," should be transferred to a setting able to provide comfort (e.g., treatment of a hip fracture).

A person who chooses either "comfort measures only" or "limited additional interventions" may not require transfer or referral to a facility with a higher level of care.

An IV medication to enhance comfort may be appropriate for a person who has chosen "Comfort Measures Only."

Treatment of dehydration is a measure which may prolong life. A person who desires IV fluids should indicate "Limited Additional Interventions" or "Full Treatment.

A patient with or without capacity or the surrogate who gave consent to this order or who is otherwise specifically authorized to do so, can revoke consent to any part of this order providing for the withholding or withdrawal of life-sustaining treatment, at any time, and request alternative treatment.

Review

This form should be reviewed periodically (consider at least annually) and a new form completed if necessary when:
    (1) The person is transferred from one care setting or care level to another, or
    (2) There is a substantial change in the person's health status, or
    (3) The person's treatment preferences change.

Revoking POLST

If the POLST becomes invalid or is replaced by an updated version, draw a line through sections A through E of the invalid POLST, write "VOID" in large letters across the form, and sign and date the form.

SAMPLE FILLED OUT
FORM 8:
DURABLE POWER OF ATTORNEY

NOTICE

(FOR DURABLE POWER OF ATTORNEY)

THE PURPOSE OF THIS POWER OF ATTORNEY IS TO GIVE THE PERSON YOU DESIGNATE (YOUR "AGENT") BROAD POWERS TO HANDLE YOUR PROPERTY, WHICH MAY INCLUDE POWERS TO SELL OR OTHERWISE DISPOSE OF ANY REAL OR PERSONAL PROPERTY WITHOUT ADVANCE NOTICE TO YOU OR APPROVAL BY YOU.

THIS POWER OF ATTORNEY DOES NOT IMPOSE A DUTY ON YOUR AGENT TO EXERCISE GRANTED POWERS, BUT, WHEN POWERS ARE EXERCISED, YOUR AGENT MUST USE DUE CARE TO ACT FOR YOUR BENEFIT AND IN ACCORDANCE WITH THIS POWER OF ATTORNEY.

YOUR AGENT MAY EXERCISE THE POWERS GIVEN HERE THROUGHOUT YOUR LIFETIME, EVEN AFTER YOU BECOME INCAPACITATED, UNLESS YOU EXPRESSLY LIMIT THE DURATION OF THESE POWERS OR YOU REVOKE THESE POWERS OR A COURT ACTING ON YOUR BEHALF TERMINATES YOUR AGENT'S AUTHORITY.

YOUR AGENT MUST ACT IN ACCORDANCE WITH YOUR REASONABLE EXPECTATIONS TO THE EXTENT ACTUALLY KNOWN BY YOUR AGENT AND, OTHERWISE, IN YOUR BEST INTEREST, ACT IN GOOD FAITH AND ACT ONLY WITHIN THE SCOPE OF AUTHORITY GRANTED BY YOU IN THE POWER OF ATTORNEY.

THE LAW PERMITS YOU, IF YOU CHOOSE, TO GRANT BROAD AUTHORITY TO AN AGENT UNDER POWER OF ATTORNEY, INCLUDING THE ABILITY TO GIVE AWAY ALL OF YOUR PROPERTY WHILE YOU ARE ALIVE OR TO SUBSTANTIALLY CHANGE HOW YOUR PROPERTY IS DISTRIBUTED AT YOUR DEATH. BEFORE SIGNING THIS DOCUMENT, YOU SHOULD SEEK THE ADVICE OF AN ATTORNEY AT LAW TO MAKE SURE YOU UNDERSTAND IT.

A COURT CAN TAKE AWAY THE POWERS OF YOUR AGENT IF IT FINDS YOUR AGENT IS NOT ACTING PROPERLY.

THE POWERS AND DUTIES OF AN AGENT UNDER A POWER OF ATTORNEY ARE EXPLAINED MORE FULLY IN 20 PA.C.S. CH. 56.

IF THERE IS ANYTHING ABOUT THIS FORM THAT YOU DO NOT UNDERSTAND, YOU SHOULD ASK A LAWYER OF YOUR OWN CHOOSING TO EXPLAIN IT TO YOU.

I HAVE READ OR HAD EXPLAINED TO ME THIS NOTICE AND I UNDERSTAND ITS CONTENTS.

Robert Dale Zane   _8-22-2015_
PRINCIPAL   **DATE**

DURABLE POWER OF ATTORNEY

I __Robert Dale Zane,__ 83 Pine Street, Kent, PA 19403 (insert name and address) make this power of attorney document as the principal and do hereby appoint as my agent __Linda Carrie Zane,__ 83 Pine Street, Kent, PA 19403 (insert the name and address of the person appointed), and I hereby give this agent all the power and authority I possess or may give and they may do any act, deed, matter, or thing as I could do if I were personally present except as limited by Pennsylvania or other law.

This power of attorney will continue to be effective even though I become incapacitated, disabled, or incompetent. This document is not affected by uncertainty if I am alive.

This instrument is effective immediately.

I agree any third party who receives a copy of this document may act under it. I agree to indemnify any third party for any claims that arise because of reliance on this power of attorney. Revocation is not effective as to a third party until they learn of the revocation.

Without limited any grant of power or authority, I specifically give my agent in this document the following power and authority:

To engage in tangible personal property transactions.

To engage in banking and financial transactions.

To engage in stock, bond and other securities transactions.

To engage in commodity and option transactions.

To engage in real property transactions.

To borrow money.

To enter safe deposit boxes.

To engage in insurance and annuity transactions.

To engage in retirement plan transactions.

To handle interests in estates and trusts.

To pursue claims and litigation.

To receive government benefits.

To pursue tax matters.

To make limited gifts.

To create a trust for my benefit.

To make additions to an existing trust for my benefit.

To claim an elective share of the estate of my deceased spouse.

To authorize my admission to a medical, nursing, residential or similar facility and to enter into agreements for my care.

To renounce fiduciary positions.

To withdraw and receive the income or corpus of a trust.

(Optional) I hereby limit or extend the power and authority given my agent in this document, which shall control over any other provision, as follows: _____

_____

_____.

PRINCIPAL

I willfully and voluntarily sign this document as principal and I understand its purpose.

Signed this _22nd_ day of __August, 2015_ .

Robert Dale Zane
_____
Principal's Signature

WITNESSES

This document was signed in our presence and the person who signed this document as principal appears to be of sound mind and to be making this designation voluntarily, without duress, fraud, or undue influence, and we sign below as witnesses.

Witness Signature: _Paul Alan Lind_   Witness Signature: _Joy Dee Pond_

Print Name: Paul Alan Lind   Print Name: Joy Dee Pond

NOTARY

On this _22nd_ day of __August, 2015_ before me personally appeared the above-named principal who is satisfactorily proven to be the person named principal, who then executed this document as principal and acknowledged doing so.

In witness whereof, I hereunto set my hand and official seals.

Nathan Oliver Notario
_____
Notary

ACKNOWLEDGMENT EXECUTED BY AGENT

I, __Linda Carrie Zane__, HAVE READ THE ATTACHED POWER OF ATTORNEY AND AM THE PERSON IDENTIFIED AS THE AGENT FOR THE PRINCIPAL. I HEREBY ACKNOWLEDGE THAT WHEN I ACT AS AGENT:

I SHALL ACT IN ACCORDANCE WITH THE PRINCIPAL'S REASONABLE EXPECTATIONS TO THE EXTENT ACTUALLY KNOWN BY ME AND, OTHERWISE, IN THE PRINCIPAL'S BEST INTEREST, ACT IN GOOD FAITH AND ACT ONLY WITHIN THE SCOPE OF AUTHORITY GRANTED TO ME BY THE PRINCIPAL IN THE POWER OF ATTORNEY.

__*Linda Carrie Zane*__   __8-22-2015__

AGENT   DATE

**SAMPLE FILLED OUT
FORM 9:
MEDICAL CONSENT AUTHORIZATION (FOR CHILD)**

MEDICAL CONSENT AUTHORIZATION
(FOR CHILD UNDER THE MEDICAL CONSENT ACT)

I __Mindy Sue Bell__ (name) am the parent of the child(ren) listed below and there are no court orders now in effect that would prohibit me from conferring the power to consent upon another person.

I, __Mindy Sue Bell__, do hereby confer upon __Harriet Vera Bell__, residing at __83 Main St., Polk, PA 18103__ the power to consent to necessary medical or mental health treatment for the following child(ren):

__Timothy Chet Bell__, residing at __223 Smith St., Polk, PA 18103__, born on __July 6, 2011__,

_____, residing at
_____, born on _____,

_____, residing at
_____, born on _____,

and on the child(ren)'s behalf do hereby state that the power to consent which I confer shall not be affected by my subsequent disability or incapacity.

The power which I confer is specifically limited to health care and mental health care decision making, and it may be exercised only by the person named above.

The person named above may consent to the child(ren)'s (cross out all that do not apply): medical, dental, surgical, developmental and/or mental health examination or treatment and may have access to any and all records, including, but not limited to, insurance records regarding any such services.

I confer the power to consent freely and knowingly in order to provide for the child(ren) and not as a result of pressure, threats or payments by any person or agency. This document shall remain in effect until it is revoked by notifying my child(ren)'s medical, mental health care and insurance providers, in writing, and the person named above that I wish to revoke it.

IN WITNESS WHEREOF, I, __Mindy Sue Bell__, have signed my named to this medical consent authorization, on this __11th__ day of __January__, 20 __16__.

Mindy Sue Bell
(Signature)

Mindy Sue Bell
(Printed Name)

Ann Kim Chomsky
(Witness Signature)

88 Hunter Street, Silver, PA 18103
(Witness No. 1 printed Name and Address)

Norm Alan Chomsky
(Witness Signature)

88 Hunter Street, Silver, PA 18103
(Witness No. 1 printed Name and Address)

ACCEPTANCE. I accept the power given in this document. Signed: _Harriet Vera Bell_

SAMPLE FILLED OUT
FORM 10:
STATEMENT OF CONTRARY INTENT (FOR BODY)

STATEMENT OF CONTRARY INTENT
(FOR BODY)

I, __Thomas Samuel Beckett__ , appoint __Mary Juliet King__ , as my agent for disposition of my body and related matters, and I give my agent and all other persons the instructions written below as authorized by 20 Pa. C. S. § 305 or other laws.

My agent shall have the sole right to determine disposition of my body after my death, including by burial, cremation, or any other form of disposition. No other person regardless of their kinship status to me or status as my spouse shall override my agent.

If I do not give instructions below to the person I appointed they still shall have the power, authority, rights, and privileges I described above and as provided them by law.

My agent shall follow instructions to the degree they can be reasonably accomplished and I have provided sufficient funds and property to pay for things (I understand I may leave areas blank):

I want to have my body handled in the following manner concerning place, coffin, shroud , cremation, embalming, container, tombstone, or similar issues:

I want an affordable funeral and burial with a simple tombstone. My agent may decide what to do.

I direct the following ceremony, service, wake, visitation, readings, events, or similar:

I have the following other instructions, requests, reminders, thanks, or similar:

(attach additional sheets as necessary)

__Thomas Samuel Beckett__   __8-22-2015__
Signature   Date

Signature of Witnesses (optional)

__Robert Dale Zane__   __Kay Paula Bing__

108

END OF BOOK

NOTES

NOTES

NOTES

WWW.DAVENPORTPRESS.ORG

GO TO

<u>WWW.DAVENPORTPRESS.ORG</u>

TO DOWNLOAD FORMS,

DOWNLOAD BOOKS,

AND GIVE COMMENTS

CPSIA information can be obtained
at www.ICGtesting.com
Printed in the USA
LVHW051417070920
665237LV00019B/2082